KETTERMAN ON KIDS

Also by Grace Ketterman on topics related to this book:

The Complete Book of Baby and Child Care

Don't Give In, Give Choices: Winning Your Child's Cooperation (with Pat Holt)

Fathering: A Practical Guide for Dads

Marriage: First Things First

Parenting the Difficult Child

Preparing for Parenthood

Surviving the Darkness (on depression)

Understanding Your Child's Problems

Verbal Abuse: Healing the Hidden Wound

When You Feel Like Screaming: Help for Frustrated Mothers (with Pat Holt)

Ketterman on

Answers to the
Questions
Parents Ask Most

Grace Ketterman, M.D.

Harold Shaw Publishers
Wheaton, Illinois

ISBN 0-87788-617-2

Edited by Joan Guest

Cover design by David LaPlaca

Library of Congress Cataloging-in-Publication Data

Ketterman, Grace H.
    [199 questions parents ask]
    Ketterman on kids : answers to questions parents ask most / Grace H. Ketterman.
    Originally published: 199 questions parents ask. Old Tappan, N.J.
    F. H. Revell, ©1986.
    Includes index.
    ISBN 0-87788-617-2
    1. Child rearing—Miscellanea. 2. Child psychology—Miscellanea.
    3. Parenting—Religious aspects—Christianity. I. Title.
    HQ769.K42 1997
    649'.1—DC2   96-17353
                                            CIP

---

03   02   01   00   99   98

10 9 8 7 6 5 4 3 2

CONTENTS

INTRODUCTION
My Basic Views on Childrearing

The shrill ringing of the telephone grated on my spirit as I began to relax at 10:00 P.M. My day had begun with a 7:30 A.M. appointment, and I had missed lunch in order to see a grandmother who was concerned about her rebellious, adolescent grandchild. Frankly, I was tempted to ignore the raucous sound, but because of the lateness of the hour, I was afraid it might be prompted by an emergency.

This call was not a true crisis, but to the anxious mother who was calling, the problem was distressing. Her preteen daughter had been increasingly moody and anxious. On this evening she had refused to go to the dark basement on an errand and now was refusing to turn out the light in her bedroom.

Only a few days before, the mother of a two year old had called me to ask if I knew of any classes she could attend to help her in parenting her difficult child. Most of the time she felt quite confident in her role as mother, but there were days, she confided, when she was so angry with her son's limit-testing and rebelliousness that she was fearful of abusing him.

I receive countless telephone calls about family matters, and for years I also received many letters asking my advice in response to my former radio program, "You and Your Child." These have made me aware of the multitudinous concerns parents share. While many of the issues are similar, each is uniquely painful to those who struggle to survive, to cope, and to resolve the problems.

The purpose of this book, then, is to capture in print the practical, to-the-point answers that seem to have helped many people. Perhaps you, too, may find the one burning concern that confronts you addressed here. I hope it will help you and your child.

Importance of Early Childhood

I want to begin this book with an outline of my basic approach to childrearing. I'm hoping that attention to these basics will help you as you journey the road of parenthood.

The first point I want to make is that the parenting role is critically important *as soon as it begins.* Whether we consider the strength of a building, the straightness of a tree, or the development of a human being, we realize the vital necessity of correctness in early building.

In early childhood, there is an irretrievable opportunity to lay solid, true foundations that will permit the construction of a sound and lovely life! It is through the establishment of *balances* that such soundness is built. The following are some of those balances:

- Enough attention and protection to establish trust, but not enough to stifle growth toward individuality and independence.

- Enough limits to offer security, but not enough to prompt rebellion or promote the despair of helplessness.

- Enough work to teach the pride of achievement, but not so much that life becomes a drudgery.

- Enough discipline and training to teach a sense of responsibility, but not so much that it destroys a sense of healthy freedom.

- Enough laughter and play to keep life joyful, but not so much that pleasure becomes a goal in itself.

- Enough consistency to make life predictable, but not so much that it makes life unbearably rigid.

- Enough pride to teach the happiness of being productive, but not so much that it makes a child an egomaniac.

- Enough love to make each day tender and warm and to motivate painful efforts when needed and for a lifetime!

The significance of training pets is well understood, and when such training is practiced, the animal is loyal and pleasurable. How much more should parents recognize that there are principles of training that apply to children as well! Deciding what you want the child to do, establishing rewards effectively, and applying firm consequences in a highly consistent manner are the primary rules for training.

Discipline Is Essential

For children training is not enough, and few people see the significant difference between training and discipline. Training is a basic, neuromuscular response that can be taught simply through rewards or punishments.

Discipline, on the other hand, is a complex teaching-learning process that involves reason and understanding. It is the process, as I see it, of learning why certain consequences go into effect, what is good or bad about certain behaviors and attitudes, and what makes them good or bad. It is the application to all of life of a few meaningful policies and philosophies. In short, good discipline results in the growth of wisdom.

It is not difficult to love most tiny babies. They are so helpless and vulnerable that even those who cry excessively are given constant attention and loving care by most parents. The first teeth, the first steps, the first words—all bring out excitement and pride from doting parents.

How different, though, is the first "No! I won't!" It is in the early search for freedom and the testing of boundaries that many lifelong battles between parents and children begin. Parents who fail to see this as a healthy component of the child's personality are likely to resent the child and establish no-win power struggles. On the other hand, they may lazily give in, permitting the child a damaging sense of power that is not founded on experience or reason.

It is not only in the balances of life that parents may win or lose the struggle for healthy child raising. It is also in their inner core of strength and their attitudes that more (or less) good building takes place. It is rarely what parents *want* for their children that is wrong, but the *methods* they employ to gain obedience that go awry.

From such experiences, conflictual or harmonious, the emotions of children are formed. When there is plenty of unconditional love and pride in the child's growing achievements, those emotions are healthy and the child's self-esteem will develop into strength. But when compassion and understanding are lacking, and when parents' disapproval and anger outweigh the communication of their love, a child's developing personality becomes blighted. Later on, serious trouble is predictable.

The Foundation and the Adolescent Years

It is in the adolescent years that the cracks in the foundation of a child's personality become clearly visible. It was, however, the family foundation of the early years that contributed to the damage.

If essential balances were not reached, and disapproval too heavily outweighed parental approval, the child lacked the proper building materials. Those hidden weaknesses now emerge in behavioral disorders that are seen by parents as rebelliousness. Actually there are three primary reasons for serious adolescent misbehaviors:

1. Parents are too rigid or strict. When parents are dictatorial and maintain too much control over too long a period of time, young people are likely to rebel in order to establish a semblance of independence. Since the job of teenagers is to do that very thing if they are to become healthy adults, parents must not only allow but *encourage* them to grow steadily toward independence, in order to avoid serious rebellion.

2. Parents are too lenient or inconsistent. Teenagers need to have their boundaries enlarged, but they still need boundaries. When parents do not establish such limits or enforce them only erratically, adolescents will test them regularly. The more erratic the parents are, the more strenuously the young people must test their limits. To stop dangerous behaviors, parents must begin to set limits and enforce them with great consistency.

3. Adolescents act out emotional pain. When teenagers feel very inadequate or carry anxieties and worries that are too heavy, they often act out such painful emotions in wildly erratic behavior. By doing drugs or carrying out antisocial acts, they can temporarily escape their pain. They may even set themselves up to get caught and punished, because punishment temporarily relieves their guilt. Such young people need a chance to explore their needs and to verbalize those painful feelings, so they will not need to act up.

Understanding teenagers is fundamental to staying in love with them, enjoying them, and seeing them through those difficult years.

Influence of Others on Teens

During these important years, the availability of the extended family is a prime benefit to both parents and adolescents. On the other hand, if relatives do not share the values of the family, or if the young person uses them to manipulate and win power struggles, relatives can create more problems than help. When parents, grandparents, and other relatives do not enjoy a really sound relationship (or are frankly at odds), such manipulations can reach dangerous proportions.

In today's rootless society, frequent moves often prevent the forming of relationships between grandchildren and grandparents or other relatives. In such situations, parents may benefit the family by looking for surrogate grandparents. Mutual enrichment may be the result. Some churches help this process by arranging mentors for young children and teens.

Tragically, there are many persons and groups in our society who relate to teenagers in a destructive alliance against the parents. Those whose values are highly permissive are an easy target for restless youth who search for permission to rebel against parents they see as old-fashioned and rigid.

Another influential factor on teens is gangs and their violence. Children in search of excitement and protection are easy prey to them. Threats and coercion by gangs play a large role in parental worries in the late 1990s. Gangs have in many communities replaced the mind-bending and financial exploitation of young people practiced by various cult groups. Cults do, however, still exist, so be alert.

Building a Sound Spiritual Foundation

A major defense against negative influences is a sound spiritual foundation. Through the practical application of their own religious beliefs and traditions, families can build into the lives of their children the basic truths by which they live. Studies have shown that such family practices create strength and promote family cohesiveness.

A child who lives with the laughter, training, and protection of a loving human father is not easily tempted by even the most charismatic of cult leaders. Rather, due to the strong foundation of love, such children find it easy as they grow older to trust the heavenly Father.

A frequent question I receive is related to the best methods for teaching spiritual values to children and helping adolescents validate their beliefs. In today's hedonistic society, there are no pat answers to that extremely important question, but here are some practical ideas which I believe can help.

- *Parents, establish your own values.* When you know what you believe and demonstrate those beliefs in your daily lives, your children will have difficulty denying those beliefs.

- *Teach your beliefs.* While verbally discussing values without living them is likely to go unheeded, living them without explaining and teaching them may allow them to be taken for granted.

- *Keep the practices of your faith joyful.* It is easy to focus on the limiting, negative rules of the Bible without teaching the protective, loving reasons for them. Simple but honest explanations are important.

- *Pray family prayers—but keep them simple.* I recommend family prayers from the wedding on—short sentences of joys shared, sorrows comforted, needs presented, hurts healed, and all of life brought regularly to the heavenly Father. From the time they can speak a few words, children should be led to pray when their families do.

- *Avoid using God as a threat or punishment.* Telling children that God will punish them for misbehaving, or stating that "God doesn't like children who . . . " will destroy their faith in the love and grace of God.

Few people can resist optimistic, welcoming, unconditional love. Even the Prodigal Son returned to his father. And sure enough, the father was waiting, looking far down the road for a glimpse of the first sign of that return. So even if your children stray, don't give up your commitment. Expect them back, and be ready to meet them when they reappear on the horizon of your hearts!

Let Go!

Every young person must grow through the developmental stages so clearly outlined by child psychologists. The temptation to cling tenaciously to your children could make them social and emotional cripples. Children are born to mature, to establish their own identities, and to separate from their families in order to establish their own homes in due time. The parents who recognize this and encourage the independence— gradually but confidently—will rarely need to suffer the heartache of serious rebellion and estrangement. With each child the transition is different, but with each it can be full of joy and love of a new and richer sort.

One of the frightening aspects of this stretch toward independence is tied to the social issues of young lives. When children are little, parents can supervise their play and other activities. If a little friend is judged to be harmful, he or she can be excluded from the home. Not so when teen years arrive! The opportunities to establish relationships in school, on jobs, and in the neighborhood simply cannot be regulated by parents.

The permissiveness of our Western culture and its relative affluence create dangers that are truly frightening. Wise parents walk a fine line of guidance that is designed to teach the emerging young adult basic principles for sound decision making. They enlarge the freedoms in proportion to the sense of responsibility they see in that young person. And they encourage him when he fails or makes less than optimal choices. They often must set some protective limits, but as much as possible, they lead their teenager to learn to manage his or her own life.

Keeping open the channels of communication is not always easy in these difficult years! But when parents believe in their own good parenting, then their adolescent's good will and desire to please them—and most of all, the transcending love of God—will see the parents through, and their child as well.

The questions that follow are actual ones that were written to me. They have been edited, and identifying information has been carefully removed or changed to protect the persons who wrote.

I hope these questions are representative of all of the people who endure such worries. And I trust that the answers, though brief, will be clear, practical, hopeful, and useful!

Note on gender pronouns: If the question did not specify that a child was a girl or a boy, the author has alternated the use of male and female pronouns in order to avoid referring to all children as boys.

1

BABY CARE

POSTPARTUM

Just what are postpartum blues?

I was taught in medical school that postpartum blues were caused by a complicated set of hormone imbalances that sometimes happen after a baby is born. Certainly the mother's body does go through many changes after the birth of a child, and a very important part of that change is the reestablishment of the normal rhythm of her hormones.

But I also think there is a form of postartum depression that is not related to hormones. A few years ago, I had a visit from a postpartum father, and he was experiencing the postpartum blues just as the same as any mother I had ever seen. As I talked with him, and subsequently with other fathers, I found that they, too, went through a time of depression and sadness after the birth of their children.

In researching this and thinking about it deeply with these fathers and mothers, I discovered some reasons that may be helpful to know.

These days most people who have a baby want that baby

very much. They want a child they can love and enjoy, and they want to show off that baby to their family and friends. During the pregnancy the mother gains a great deal of attention, and the father is excited about watching the movement of the baby, and feeling it inside the mother's body. Those bodily changes, the developing baby, the fixing up of the room, the parties and the showers, and the anticipation are all very much in high gear for expectant parents.

But after that long nine-month wait, suddenly the baby is there. The parties are over, the room is fixed up, but the occupant of that room can become a tyrant, and parents can get worn-out, tired. They had not realized ahead of time how much of their freedom they were going to have to give up. The facts that become increasingly clear to the new parents are these: *We have lost our freedom.* Or, if it's a subsequent child, *we have lost more freedom than we lost before. We have assumed a heavy responsibility 24 hours a day, 365 days a year, for a lifetime. We risk the loss of each other's attention. We have financial burdens in supplying the needs that are, frankly, mind-boggling. Furthermore, it's inconvenient to deal with dirty diapers and getting up at night!*

Few parents are truly prepared for giving up so many freedoms and assuming so many responsibilities. It's no surprise then that when these realizations accumulate suddenly for either father or mother, there is a time of grieving and sadness. The positive part of all of this is that grief is a well-known process. You can recover from it and learn to truly appreciate that little bundle of joy that has come to enrich your lives—as well as to create some responsibilities for you as parents.

NEW-BABY SUPPLIES

What clothes and equipment will our new infant

require during those first few days at home? Please limit the list to the basics a new baby needs.

The basics really are fairly simple, but I would like to start with one that I think is most important, and that is a *rocking chair.* Rocking chairs may have gone out of vogue in many families, but the ability to hold a child and provide the rhythmic motion that the baby really has been accustomed to within the mother's body is very soothing to both child and parent.

Obviously your baby will need a *bed* on which to lie, and many parents feel they need a series of beds (a bassinet, a portable crib, a baby bed), but really you need only one, the crib. The crib should have a firm mattress that will provide good support to the baby's body. You must be very careful that the bars on the sides of that crib are close enough that the baby's head cannot get wedged between the bars. (All new cribs are required to have bars this close.) I recommend that the bed be equipped with a *bumper pad.* You can make that yourself from a long strip of cardboard with some padding and a bit of bright fabric, or you can purchase one that coordinates with the crib sheets. A bumper pad helps to protect your child's head from bumping the sides of the crib.

You will also need some *pads* and *sheets* for the bed. I suggest some small waterproof pads. Then you don't have to launder the entire linen supply every day, but can simply wash the little pads that will keep the moisture off the sheet if the child's wet diaper doesn't contain it all. I do *not* recommend a pillow until the child is old enough to move the head well. Babies can get their noses tucked into that soft pillow and actually suffocate.

You will certainly need a great many *diapers,* because your baby's bladder will function very well! Cloth diapers still are cheaper to use than disposable ones, but there is a great deal of time and energy spent in laundering them. If you prefer a diaper service, then the cost will be about the same as disposables. You, as parents, need to decide what your time and financial resources are. If you decide on cloth diapers, you will need at least three dozen in order to meet the needs of the baby while not constantly doing laundry. If you have a relative who asks you for a gift suggestion, tell him or her to give you either disposable diapers or a diaper service for the first six weeks of your baby's life!

If you use cloth diapers, a few *plastic pants* to put over the baby's diaper will help prevent a soggy bed and a soggy baby, thus reducing your laundry needs.

Also important are baby clothes: *undershirts,* at least three; three or four baby *gowns* with cuffs that can encase their fists to avoid scratching and drawstrings to encase the feet to keep them warm. If your home is cool on winter nights, get warm *blanket sleepers* for the baby to wear at night, as the crib blanket will not stay on Baby for long.

A couple of light *receiving blankets* and one larger, warmer *crib blanket* complete the list of bare essentials. Babies really do not need very much equipment. What they do need is a great deal of loving attention from you, the parents!

Breastfeeding is the most beneficial way to nourish your baby, but if you breastfeed you must be prepared for a struggle the first week or two. Babies do have a natural instinct to suck, but it is a lot of work for them. And in the early days the baby may be too sleepy to feed very much. Meanwhile, the mother's milk comes in and she can become engorged, making it hard for the baby to grasp the nipple. If you want to breastfeed, make sure your pediatrician is supportive of that, and ask the hospital to refrain from giving a bottle. If you can persevere through the initial difficult days, you may well find breastfeeding a tremendously rewarding experience. In many cities, local mothers' groups assist new moms with breastfeeding by answering their questions and providing encouragement. Ask your pediatrician about such groups in your locality. The only equipment that breastfeeding mothers need is a *maternity bra* or two, a couple of *nightgowns* that allow you to feed the baby without undressing, and perhaps a *cream* for sore nipples.

Since not everyone can or wants to breastfeed, there are a variety of *bottles* to choose from, including several with tips that closely resemble the feel of a natural nipple. For ease in cleaning, I would recomend a system that uses disposable plastic bags. That way you do not have to worry about sanitizing anything other than the nipple for your baby.

NAMING YOUR CHILD

What suggestions do you have for parents who are deciding on names for their baby?

This is one of the more pleasant tasks that expectant parents face. In the Bible it is clear that names were given considerable thought. God revealed to the patriarchs many times what they were to name their children, and those names meant a great deal. Family names sometimes are important. For instance, some fathers would like to have a son named after themselves, a grandfather, or a great-grandfather. Sometimes families would like to name a child after a relative, friend, or historical figure who means a lot to them. The name a child is given does have great significance. There are many name books available that give the meaning of the various choices.

Be aware also that your child will probably be given a nickname at some point. So, when you consider names, also consider the various short forms. They should not be names that would insult or humiliate your child. And be sure you remember to always use your child's name with love, whatever name you may choose.

BABY'S LAUNDRY

What special care does a baby's laundry call for?

That is an important question, because most babies have tender skin and some of their diapers and linens are extremely difficult to get clean. Every mother wants nice white, bright clothes for her little baby, and the sense of her adequacy as a mother may even depend on the condition of that linen! On the other hand, stains are the norm for babies. Urine and bowel movements stain sheets and pants, and what babies spit up can make their best bibs and shirts look dreadful. Orange juice and many baby foods leave difficult stains.

Harsh bleaches and detergents create white, bright linens, and fabric softeners make things fluffy, but they also may irritate a baby's tender skin, causing more rashes than you can clear up in a month's time! Here are my suggestions for laundering your child's linens and preventing irritations on that delicate skin:

Rinse all soiled fabrics at once in cool water. Hot water can set certain stains, so avoid hot water, but do use plenty of cool water. Then I recommend using an enzyme solution. These come under many trade names, but they will advertise themselves clearly as to their effectiveness in taking care of a variety of stains. You will find that soaking your baby's linens and clothing in that enzyme solution will be magical. It simply dissolves away the protein substances that create the stains, and yet it does not hurt the fabric and is harmless to your child's skin. After rinsing in this special solution, I would rinse in clear water again.

Now run the clothes through your washing machine with a very mild detergent. Most fabrics for children are now made of flame-retardant materials. These items must be washed in detergent, not soap, to retain their effectiveness. Read the detergent labels and choose the one that seems safest for babies. (Some detergents come with no perfume or dye additives.) If your child gets a rash, use a second rinse cycle. *Avoid bleaches.*

Fabric softeners are sometimes helpful in making clothes and diapers soft, but those that are put in with the clothes in the dryer leave a residue that can irritate sensitive skin. Use a fabric softener in the washer instead. There are special dispensers that will distribute the softener at the right time so you don't have to catch the washer at the right point in the cycle. Occasionally, a baby may react to the scent that is put in fabric softeners, but most children will tolerate it. If not, simply select an unscented type.

After *washing, dry* the clothes. I still like clothes that are hung outside and bleached by the sunshine. If you live in an area where that is not possible, a dryer is just fine.

Keeping your baby sweet and soft and clean is one of the joys of being a good parent!

NEWBORN'S CRYING

What's the most common reason for a baby's cry?

Frankly, most babies cry in pain, but there are many other reasons for their crying. One of the worst fears of new parents is that they won't be able to stop their baby's crying. We instinctively want to soothe and comfort a baby, and when we can't, it makes us feel most inadequate.

I can so vividly recall the birth of our first baby, and how anxious I was about her cries. Having just finished medical school, I was acutely aware of all the serious medical problems possible, and every time she cried, I was certain that she had some dreadful defect or disease that ordinary parents don't have to worry about. I found, fortunately, that her cries were usually very simple, very understandable, and relatively easy to cure.

The first cry of a newborn baby is that of *pain*—the pain of being born into a rather cold and sometimes cruel world. The cry that is in response to pain may sound angry, and it is intense. The baby's fists usually double up and draw in toward the body. The eyes squeeze tightly shut, and the cry is indeed a loud and piercing cry. Being hungry, cold, wet, having an earache, a painful diaper rash—these are all conditions that can cause that angry cry in response to the indignations that life heaps upon the child.

Still other kinds of crying, however, are those of *loneliness, boredom,* or even perhaps *fear.* The lonely or bored cry is more of a whining, fretful one that can in its own turn be quite irritating to parents. And we know that even newborn babies startle with loud noises or a jolt, and this can cause a different kind of cry and a different body language. Their hands and feet extend, and their eyes open wide. Then they may come out with a very loud cry, but it has a different quality from the angry, painful cry.

Once the baby is a few months old, responding too soon to a baby's cry can actually teach a child to cry for attention. On the other hand, by responding too late or too little, you may teach the baby to become angry, or even to withdraw in silence. So, it is important that you respond appropriately, neither too soon nor too little.

You will learn to identify your child's cry and check out your baby's needs. Is her diaper wet? Could she be hungry? Does she need cuddling or attention? By providing that attention before the baby begins to cry, you may teach that little one to respond to you lovingly and positively, with less irritable crying. One of the greatest joys for a parent is the power to soothe a frightened, hungry, or hurting baby. I wish that joy for each of you.

WAKING UP BABY

Sometimes when I come home late, after a long day

at work, I'm disappointed to discover that my three-month-old son is sleeping. I'm often tempted to wake him, just to play and be friendly, and I admit sometimes I've done just that. Is it harmful to interrupt his sleep like this? If I don't, I could go days without seeing him when he's awake.

By all means, awaken the baby and enjoy him to your heart's content. He needs the bonding with both his parents, whether they work or not. Dads, for instance, may have a different approach with children, and they can help to balance out what mothers provide. Enjoy your little boy. I recommend that you change his diaper and clean him up. Feed him and play with him, and then put him back to bed.

If one of you works and the other stays home, you may find that the homebound parent is exhausted at the end of the day. Thus, if the working parent awakens the baby, that parent should also take care of the baby's needs (such as feeding or changing the diaper) and get him back to sleep. Realize that the parent at home faces as long and demanding a day ahead as does the working parent.

As soon as a baby comes, spouses should work out a schedule for sharing household tasks. The parent at home should not be stuck with all the childcare and all the domestic duties. If both parents work, then sharing all the chores is absolutely *essential.*

I also recommend that you both be aware of *each other's* need to be enjoyed, too. Be friendly and playful together with the child, and then when the child has settled down, make time to keep the romance healthy between the two of you. The best gift you can give your child is a mother and father who truly love one another. But you will have to work hard to keep that love alive. As children grow, it becomes harder and harder for Mom and Dad to find time together. Make such time a regular part of your routine by having a baby sitter scheduled at least once a week so you can get away together.

FIGHTING SLEEP

I'm wondering why it's so hard for children to go to sleep. If they are really tired, as my three-month-old daughter seems to be at times, why do they fight sleep? Is there anything we can do to help our daughter drop off to sleep more easily?

That's an important question, because parents certainly need their rest, and I know they are anxious for this three-month-old baby to sleep a little more. Some babies, of course, have trouble sleeping because of noise. A barking dog or a car honking outside, a loud radio or television can keep them awake, or awaken them as they are just drifting off.

However, most children are not bothered by noise but may be affected by overstimulation. Some children are born with a keen sense of hearing, sight, and touch, and all kinds of things bother them that would not bother a less sensitive child. These children may have difficulty screening out background noise and calming themselves down.

Sometimes new babies, particularly first ones, have overreactive parents. I once was called upon to make a house call by a set of parents whose child was crying himself into a state of hysteria. When I walked into the house I found two sets of grandparents and two parents extremely upset. I carefully examined the child and thought he must have a severe earache, but both eardrums were just fine. There was no sore throat, no fever, no rash, simply nothing to account for the child's anxious crying. I asked the parents to leave the room and give me a bottle and a rocking chair, which they very gladly did. As I sat with the child and rocked him gently for a moment, he promptly fell off to sleep. My diagnosis in that case was too many anxious relatives. Parents are bound to become concerned and tense when a child cries, and their tension can be contagious to the little one.

So, learn to relax and practice calmness when you hold your child. "Think Calm" might be a nice motto for you to put on the baby's crib. Keep the baby's environment as peaceful as you can. Dim lights, soft colors, soft music in the background—these are the things that can help your child relax. Avoid handling the baby too much, especially if you are tired or tense. If the baby is going to fuss anyway, she may be better off doing so in her crib where she can relax against the firmness of her mattress if the only alternative is being held by a frantic, nervous parent.

BORED BABY

We're new parents, and our question is this: Our daughter is two months old and very active and alert. She loves to coo and smile. She sleeps through the night and is awake most of the day. What bothers me is that sometimes she seems bored. What should we be doing to help her grow and learn? Can we spoil her with too much attention?

I'm sorry to say this question reflects a concern that a great many young parents have. There is so much emphasis on learning in our society, that many parents are more worried than they need to be about teaching even tiny babies. I wonder if this two month old is really bored or if she is exhibiting drowsiness or contentment. Perhaps it is the parents' worry that is concerning them more than the child's actual needs. This baby sounds loved and well attended. So I'd frankly hate for the parents to develop a habit of entertaining the child all of the time and trying to keep her excited or happy constantly.

Here are some suggestions for taking care of a tiny baby: After a nap pick the child up and play with her as long as you like. Feed her if she's hungry, change her diaper, and then set her down in her bed, in a playpen, or even on a blanket on the floor (if you don't have pets or other young children who might bother her). As soon as Baby can get into it without discomfort, I like the infant swings that can be placed in a room with the family. This sets the stage for a normal family life, where children observe and learn from observing, and where parents can pursue some of their own individual activities. When she is able to grasp, offer her a soft baby rattle or other such toy. Put up a mobile that can move about and attract the child's attention; also consider musical toys or bright objects tied onto the sides of her crib. Just make sure these are tied securely with short, bright ribbon instead of string, which can wrap around a baby's neck, and remove such items when Baby begins to sit up, as anything hanging across the crib can be dangerous if fallen on.

Enjoy your child, but don't become her slave. Entertain her all you like, but don't feel that you must keep her happy twenty-four hours a day. There is an intuitive, instinctive sense that parents were given to help them recognize a child's need. Follow that intuition and you can't go too far wrong.

BABY TEMPERAMENTS

My second child seemed immediately different from my first from the day he was born. This was surprising to me. Is that normal?

It certainly is normal. In fact, research has even been done on infant temperaments. Doctors Stella Chess and Alexander Thomas studied many newborns, following their lives for years. They discovered that all babies are born with nine personality traits, the degrees of which varied from slight to intense. These traits are

- activity level
- intensity level
- distractibility
- predictability
- persistence
- sensitivity level (touch, smell, taste, hearing, speech)
- approach/withdrawal
- adaptability
- mood

Some children at birth are on the low end of certain of these qualities, while others are on the high end, and most are in between. Keeping these traits in mind will help you understand and respond well to your child.

Depending on your own levels of intensity in each of these categories, your child may bring you more or less frustration. If you are basically a low-activity level person, and your child is highly active, you may find yourself worn out by the end of the day. What's important is that you accept your child as he or she is, adapt the best you can, and teach your child to modify behaviors as much as possible. Meanwhile, keep loving that baby unconditionally.

THE FUSSY, NAPLESS BABY

My little five-month-old baby has never taken a decent nap. She'll sleep for half an hour to forty-five minutes at the longest, and after this she is awake for three hours before she'll take another half-hour nap. In between naps she's usually fussy and seems

tired. This goes on every day. It's very tiring and wearing on me, because it doesn't give me a good break to get anything done. How can I get her into a better nap schedule?

This parent has a problem, and it becomes a vicious cycle. The more babies fuss and cry and the more tired mothers become, the more tense the mother feels; the baby then feels Mother's tension and cries all the more. You can easily see how this happens, so please do not blame yourself or feel guilty because you have a tense, rather sleepless child.

Sleeplessness in infants can be due to discomfort or what we have commonly called *colic.* Or it can be due to habits or to tension. These children sometimes become a bit hyperactive as they grow older.

First, make sure that there are no physical causes for the baby's sleeplessness. If you suspect that your baby may have a digestive problem, I recommend that you ask your pediatrician to help you. Giving a different formula or adjusting the feeding schedule or giving some medicated drops for gastrointestinal spasms (which may be at least a part of colic) can each be a miracle cure for some of these "difficult" babies.

Second, try to keep yourself calm, relaxed, and as happy as you possibly can, even with this irritable little one. Make the environment of the baby's nursery as calm as possible. Then, I would suggest this: Do not feel that you have to comfort, hold, or cuddle a crying baby all the time! If you can comfort the baby for five, ten, or even fifteen minutes, that's fine, but then put her back down and get on with other activities for a while. If she is still fussing, check on her and try to comfort her again. If you hold the baby for an hour, and she is still fussing, you will become more and more tense yourself. Let her cry for a time in her bed while you take a break. Then when the baby sleeps, get some rest yourself. Be comforted, because after a while the baby will quit the crying, and you will be able to enjoy each other, I assure you!

SMALL NIGHT PERSON

My daughter and her husband are thrilled with their seven-month-old little boy. They both work, but they have a lovely woman to baby-sit, so he has excellent care. His naps are short in the daytime, but he's a happy baby and the picture of health. They bathe him in the evening and play with him. The problem is his sleeping patterns at night. He can go to bed around nine, then awaken every two hours or more throughout the night. His doctor says to just let him cry it out. What can be done for a baby who keeps waking up?

Such nights are hard. Before we get to the solutions, however, let's talk first about the reasons little babies cry during the night.

Causes: There are several causes, and all of these need to be checked out. *Hunger* is certainly one of them, and little children do digest their food at various rates, so that some children need food more often than others. They may have *pain: an earache, or a stomachache,* or a variety of pains, any of which can cause them to waken and be restless at night. More often, though, a chronic problem of this sort is simply a *habit.* This child's physician seems to believe that in his case it *is* a habit. It sounds as if he has checked out all of those other possibilities. The child may also be *overly fatigued.* A baby who is played with hard and long might not be able to relax. He is overstimulated. Or, the parents, from lack of sleep, may be fatigued and short tempered. The baby will pick this up and become upset.

Solution: In the evening, follow active play with *soothing, quiet times. Delay* the bedtime a bit until the child has a proper balance of good healthy fatigue—without being exhausted—and some relaxation. Have his *room dark* and quiet, except for low, steady music or some other *monotonous sound* that will cloud the peripheral noises.

Then, if the baby wakes up and cries or does not go to sleep right away, follow the doctor's advice. I also recommend *letting the baby cry,* but with *reassuring visits* from Mom or Dad. If you check on the baby (without picking him up) every fifteen minutes or so, you communicate a sense of security—the baby is not being abandoned. You can expect the first night that he'll cry for half an hour or more. The next night about half that long, and the third night perhaps not at all. If you give the baby plenty of attention during the day, then he will not feel neglected nor abandoned at night. Teaching babies to respect their parents' needs must begin early. And you'll all be glad you did it.

BREASTFEEDING AND SOLIDS

This is a two-part question. First, when would you advise adding solid food to breastfeeding? Second, how long should I breastfeed after solid food is added regularly?

There is a wide range of advice in this area, which can confuse parents. If you happen to have a pediatrician who was trained some time ago, he or she will probably start the child on some solid foods as early as six or eight weeks. More recently, however, there is concern in medical circles about starting solid foods too soon, because we are seeing a great many children who have food allergies. My frank opinion is that it is wise to wait until the child is three or four or even six months of age before you add solid foods to the diet. The longer wait could be especially important if your family has a history of food allergies.

Let's discuss *how to add solid foods,* because that's very important. It is essential that you start with simple, single foods and none of the fancy mixtures that sound so appealing to parents. I suggest starting a baby on rice cereal, fixed with water or breast milk you have expressed. After three to six days on a little of the rice cereal, fixed according to the directions on the package, you might choose to start bananas, which are a very simple, easily digested food. Almost all babies tolerate them well and enjoy them very much. I suggest then that you add a yellow or orange-colored vegetable, such as carrots or squash. Add a single, simple meat, such as chicken, and then go back through the list again, adding another cereal, another fruit, another vegetable, until your child has had a variety of the foods that would be appealing to you (and probably will also appeal to your child).

Another very important question is *when to wean.* Some mothers prefer breastfeeding for as long as a year and a half or two years, or as long as the child wants to breastfeed. Others feel that the child should stop by nine months or whenever he begins to cut teeth. Again, this is largely a private matter, and I don't think anyone has the right to dictate exactly when a child should be weaned. However, most children in my experience (and all of my three) chose to give up their nursing at about seven to nine months of age. Frankly, I was a little disappointed! I enjoyed breastfeeding a great deal. But they would have no more of it. Though I was not able to breastfeed my children after that time, I did give them their bottle and that was a time for cuddling, holding, and rocking.

Watch your own child's body. When that child is ready to stop the sucking and oral satisfaction of nursing (or bottle feeding), allow the child to give it up. The child's own body and system knows when the time is right. Some children move right from breastfeeding to a cup or sipper cup. If you wait too long, it may be very difficult for the child to give up that sucking reflex and the need for oral satisfaction may become a habit!

WHO HOLDS THE BABY?

My question is, should young children be allowed to hold and carry babies? Also, could you suggest a diplomatic way for a parent to say no to another person who suggests letting her child hold your baby?

Babies are not toys to be dragged around like rag dolls, and yet they need a great deal of attention and stimulation. Here are some suggestions that I think will help:

First, let's consider the *intimate family members.* This mother has an only child, so he doesn't have older brothers or sisters, but many families do. Older siblings need a sense of belonging to the new baby, so they won't have the rivalry or jealousy that so often spoils their relationship. I recommend that older children be allowed and even encouraged to hold and play with a new baby. If the sibling is little (two or three years of age), certainly the parents need to be there all of the time to support the baby's head and to guide the older brother or sister in exactly how to handle and play with that little baby. Older children, of course, can learn that quite quickly, and it will be a wonderful lesson for them in child care to be given some responsibility for a new baby.

Children *outside of the family* are another problem, how-ever, since usually you do not know their overall health, general hygiene, or experience with children. I suggest that with other children (or even other adults) you give guidance and direction. If you are not comfortable with others taking your child, hold your baby in your own arms very firmly and ask them if they would like to touch your baby. Show younger children how to touch the baby's hands or stroke the baby's head or in some way get a feel of the child without taking over the handling of the baby in a way that could be risky.

With adults, you may want to say, "I hope you will enjoy our baby, but we've waited a long time for his birth, and so I'm not comfortable letting other people hold him right now."

ROCK TO SLEEP?

> **Our twin boys are now eight months old and are very good-natured and easy to take care of. They seem to feel quite secure. In the past, I've made it a point to rock them and sing them to sleep, both at naptime and nighttime. Many of my friends tell me that I should just put them down and let them cry themselves to sleep. I've tried this now for about two weeks, but they've both become very whiny and will cry for long periods. I'd appreciate your help. It would make me a more relaxed mother to know I'm doing the right thing.**

I think this mother is doing best when she or her husband rocks these little children before bed. Prior to a year or year and a half, little children seem to need the security of that holding and cuddling and rocking before going to sleep for the night. Little children at this age can't talk, and all they can do to express their needs is to cry and whine, as they are doing. By this whining they're letting their parents know that their needs have not been met. These children don't sound as if they're spoiled at all. The truly spoiled child needs a little different handling. For that manipulative child, I would recommend just putting him to bed and letting him cry, checking on him every few minutes just to let him feel secure. But by this mother's description, I feel that these children need their mother, and I would strongly urge her, even though it is a bit burdensome, to go ahead with the loving, cuddling process at bedtime. Dad's strong arms are also highly comforting to Baby, and chances are he can readily and equally participate in the bedtime routine.

THUMB SUCKING

I have a six-month-old girl who has sucked her thumb since I brought her home from the hospital. She was quite a colicky baby, and the only thing that seemed to comfort her was her thumb. People have told me to put a mitt on her hand, but what is so terrible about a baby sucking her thumb?

This is an age-old problem. Most parents who have a thumb-sucking child are worried about that child's teeth. The old worries about teeth are not necessarily true, however. In fact, dentists with whom I have consulted tell me not to worry about children who suck their thumbs, at least until the permanent teeth erupt, and then only if the child pushes very hard with the thumb against the erupting teeth. Since parents and grandparents are going to worry about thumb sucking, however, let me make some suggestions.

It is easier to prevent thumb sucking than to cure it. The suggestion given to this mother of putting a mitt on the hand would have worked had she tried that right from the hospital. Some babies' gowns have long sleeves that are made so that they will fold over the child's hands. Pacifiers, in my experience, are good ways of preventing thumb sucking. Unlike the thumb, a pacifier can be removed when the child no longer needs it.

If a baby never finds the thumb, then certainly she can't miss it later on. However, if the child is colicky and fussy, there is often a need to have the comfort and reassurance of that little thumb in her mouth. Frankly, I agree with this mother. I do not think that it is so terrible.

However, if there is a problem (and perhaps your mother or an aunt is telling you to make that child quit sucking her thumb), you may try some of these ideas:

1. Allow plenty of nursing time when the baby is feeding, so that she may fall asleep without the need to suck her thumb.

2. At this age (six months), be sure she has safe toys to hold, so that she can entertain herself or put the toy in her mouth to chew on. You must be very careful not to give the child something she could choke on or put too far into her mouth. Focus the child's waking attention on objects outside of her own body. A cradle gym, a musical toy, or a mobile can entertain the child, and she will reach for those objects rather than for her own mouth.

3. Play with your child and teach her to use her hands for activities other than thumb sucking.

4. Finally, try a pacifier if the baby will take it. As I've already said, it is easier to wean a child from a pacifier, which can be taken away, than from a thumb, which is always available.

TO BURP OR NOT TO BURP

It seems that the older our son gets—he's three months—the more he is spitting up. Should we be burping him more often to prevent this, or is it natural for him to be spitting up more as he grows older?

In a number of children there is a relaxed valve that opens into a baby's stomach. As the baby becomes more active and starts squirming and kicking, he simply squeezes out the contents of the stomach and then spits them out. It isn't serious, and rarely does the child spit up enough to cause a problem with weight gain; but it can be most annoying to parents.

In a case of severe spitting up, burping will help only slightly. By removing gas bubbles and helping to relax a fairly full little tummy, you may prevent some of the spitting up, but it won't stop it altogether. When this child grows a little bit older, becomes even more active, and starts flopping over on his tummy, his problem may become worse again. However, as soon as the child starts standing up and walking, the problem will disappear almost overnight. Until that time, here are some suggestions:

Keep a large supply of bibs. Keeping a bib around the child's neck will catch most of the spill-overs, and those bibs can be changed easily and eliminate having to launder the baby's entire outfit.

Be patient. That's perhaps the most important thing I can tell you. Your baby is not doing this intentionally.

Consider shifting the crib mattress. Once in a while I have seen a baby whose spitting up was so severe that to keep him from losing weight the parents had to prop up the bed. Wooden blocks that fit snugly under the head end of the baby's bed and will not slip can be used to elevate the bed. The force of gravity will keep the baby from spitting up so much. Many cribs also come with brackets that allow you to adjust the height. On these cribs, you can simply set the head-end brackets higher than the feet.

You should consult your pediatrician if your child has a serious degree of this problem. I can tell you, however, I have never seen a kindergartener spit up. You and your child will survive this annoying habit.

EARLY WALKERS

A friend of mine has a baby who never crawled, but went directly to walking using a walker. Is that advisable?

We know that some learning-disabled children have gone through their early developmental stages without crawling. There are those who believe that crawling is an essential stage of a child's motor and neurological development. If your child is trying to walk without having learned to crawl, you can intervene. Get down on the floor with your little pretoddler, and crawl with the child. Not only is it fun but it also develops that child's body in a fashion that seems to have a great influence on later learning capacities.

TOILET TRAINING

Would you please review for me your suggestions for toilet training? It's been a while since I've had to go through this, and I need some help remembering what to do.

Whether you have one child or a dozen, it seems as though every time you face toilet training, it's a new challenge. It is one of the most common problems that I receive letters about, and I'm glad to repeat my advice for this mother. I urge parents not to feel rushed or anxious. Only children with serious neurological damage fail to master this physical skill, and I find that most problems in toilet training come from overanxious parents. So relax. Watch your child for readiness to begin. Don't go by someone else's arbitrary recommendation that because he is two years old, he should begin toilet training. It simply doesn't work that way.

Certain signs will help you know that your child is ready for toilet training. These are as follows:

1. The child has *dry periods of over an hour.* When he awakens dry after a nap or in the morning, the child may be aware that he is ready to begin using the potty.

2. The child shows that he is *aware of the process* of urination (e.g., when he looks at his diaper while urinating).

When your child shows these signs, begin educating the child. Set him on the potty. I recommend that you use a small potty chair (not a device that fits onto a toilet). Sitting on the low chair feels safer and more secure for a little child. When the child is sitting on the potty, turn on the water in the bathroom, give the child a drink of water, and even let a little warm water flow over the genital area. Many times that will be just enough to start the flow of urine, and the child will be surprised at his success (and certainly you will be delighted!).

Wait a few minutes if this does not work and let him try again. But don't keep the child on the potty so long that he becomes tired or resistant. Let him get up, put him in training pants, or even stay in the bathroom with him while he has no pants on and try again in a little while. If you have the time and want to do it, you may even spend a day in the bathroom, letting the child run about and play rather normally and then catching him when he begins to urinate. With the potty so close, he will quickly get the idea, and many parents have found that this really works quite well with their children. If you don't have a whole day to spend, however, be patient. Keep training pants on the child, rather than a diaper. This feels different, and it reminds the child to take care of his wetting in the bathroom, rather than letting it happen in the pants.

Above all, avoid scolding and punishment. When the child is ready, he will use the toilet—unless he is so tense, angry, or frightened that he simply cannot. When he does have success, praise him sincerely. If he has none in a week or ten days, I would recommend that you suspend toilet training until the child is a bit older. With patience and love your child will become toilet trained.

VACATION AND BABY

We have a seven-month-old daughter who is our delight. We have planned a one-week trip at the end of this month, when our daughter will be seven and a half months. We have tentative plans to ask one set of grandparents to take care of her for two days, and the other grandparents for six days. She doesn't cry when we leave her at either of our parents, but we are still having second thoughts about leaving her.

I certainly urge young parents to get away now and then. The most precious gift you can give your child is loving one another and keeping your romance alive as husband and wife. I know that time alone is very precious. But at your daughter's age (just seven months), I would advise against a long trip. The child may very well enjoy her grandparents for a period of some hours, or even a day or two, but a week is quite a long time for a child of her age. Studies have been done, in fact, that indicate that children under a year of age may become depressed and feel abandoned when their parents are away from them for as long as a week. After about eighteen months, harm is much less likely, as the child seems to understand that people leave and come back. An older child can accept a parent's leaving and survive comfortably.

Perhaps for this vital first year, you could settle for a long weekend, rather than an entire week or eight days. However, if you do decide to go ahead and try this week away or if you haven't any choice, let me recommend the following. Have the little girl go and spend a night or two with each of the grandparents before you go. Picking her up and bringing her back to her own home will allow her to know that she has not been abandoned and that you will come back for her. As the child then spends longer times with those grandparents, she will be able to tolerate it, I hope, without anxiety.

QUALITY TIME

How much time should a parent spend with her baby and toddler? I'm speaking of quality time during the day. How can parents tell if they're spending too much or too little time with their child?

That concern is a valid one, because I know parents, especially those who do not work outside the home, can feel trapped at times and need to get away. Most parents can spend as much time as possible with their children, unless they begin to feel tense and frustrated. If parent and child come to be at odds with one another and are miserable, they will be better off if the parent gets away and finds a little freedom and relaxation on a regular basis. Then that parent can come back and truly enjoy the child. If a child becomes overly dependent and whiny, or acts spoiled, then the parents may be giving in too much to him and building their world entirely around him. If a child becomes clingy and acts frightened, or perhaps withdrawn and emotionally cold, then perhaps the parents are spending too little time with him. In an older child, regression to bed-wetting, thumb sucking, or other childish habits may be an indication that the parents' time or the quality of that time is lacking.

What is *quality time?* Perhaps that answer will also help this mother. I think quality time is time that is *focused* on relaxing and enjoying the child. Playing together happily, attending to his needs, teaching and guiding, cuddling and cooing, laughing and talking together. Those are things that happy parents and well-adjusted children enjoy. Quality time is time freely given because of proper priorities. Perhaps a neat house will not take a great deal of time, but a deeply cleaned house may, and it can wait. Reasonable meals without compulsion for elaborate or gourmet menus will spare a lot more time for fun with the child. I hope that the quality and the enjoyment of your time with your child will grow as he does.

With more parents in the workforce, either out of necessity or desire, *quality time* has become a way of justifying being away from home for long hours. Working mothers, for example, are told it's the *quality* of the time with the child, not the *quantity* that counts. The best research, however, as cited in Burton White's *The First Three Years of Life,* indicates that babies do best in every way when they are cared for by a biological parent most of the time up to at least the age of three.

When your child is able to entertain himself for a few minutes, allow him to do so. Place him near you as you work, talk to him, smile at him, and touch him now and then. Such actions will encourage a healthy amount of self-entertainment to balance your focused attention to him.

Remember, if you must work away from home, keep your household tasks to a minimum and spend as much of your time as possible with your children. Find mutually enjoyable activities, play and laugh together, teach and train them well! All too soon they will be independent. *Then* you can clean house, put your career on the fast track, or whatever you like.

SECURITY BLANKET

I have a question about my seven-month-old daughter. When she was three months old, someone gave her a very soft blanket made out of a silky material. She likes it so much that she absolutely will not go to sleep without it, and it has to be over her head. Is this normal, or should I try to get her to not be so attached to this blanket?

Actually this baby is in good company, because most children become attached to some form of security blanket. Children need object constancy, and that means that they need something that is going to be consistently and absolutely the same, day after day after day. It is the sameness that seems to offer such children the security or sense of safety that they need. In fact, that's how the name *security blanket* came about.

Children are strange little bundles of receptor nerves. They pick up all kinds of impulses from the environment about them. They are highly sensitive to anything that acts upon those nerve endings, and touch is especially important in tiny babies. Smell, sight, and hearing are important as well. As children grow and become interested in their external world, they lose interest in the attachments they have formed with objects and their own bodies, such as thumbs, security blankets, or teddy bears. Tucking those things away too soon or worrying about them excessively simply creates insecurity, which is often expressed through whining, crying, or nervous habits.

I strongly recommend that this child be allowed to have that blanket. I would even recommend that you take good care of it, so that it will last long enough to go through the stage in which she does need it! Eventually, of course, you will wean her from it. You will need to take it away from her to wash it now and then, because with the hard wear they get, security blankets become very soiled. I would suggest that you substitute other soft or silky items for the particular blanket that the child likes. Have her take something else along to bed, so that she won't have just one item to become attached to. Since this child is only seven months old, she will have quite a period of time to use that particular item. I wonder if this mother might not want to purchase another blanket very similar, because she will become troubled (and needlessly so) if she doesn't have something that meets that need.

If the blanket is large, this mother might want to cut it into two or three pieces so there is always a piece left if one gets lost. Also, small babies can get wound up in blankets and suffocate if the blanket is tight over the face. So, if your baby has a large blanket, check to be sure she does not pull it over her face.

Someday, shred by shred, that blanket will wear away. If your child is twelve to eighteen months or older, I would let that happen. Substitute your presence for the blanket. Your cuddling and stroking of the child will get her through that loss with minimum grief. Both she and you will survive the loss of that security blanket when that must happen.

2

TODDLERS AND PRESCHOOLERS

EARLY DISCIPLINE

I would appreciate any help you can offer concerning the discipline of a child between one and two years of age.

The key to good discipline of a child of any age is a clear understanding of the behavior of which that boy or girl is capable. And it's especially important to keep that in mind when you are dealing with a very young child.

There is a term that refers to a form of discipline used with toddlers. It is *environmental discipline,* otherwise known as *child-proofing a home.* This means changing the environment so the child cannot get into trouble. It refers to using gates, cabinet locks, outlet covers, high shelves and other strategies that protect a very young child from his investigative impulses.

Environmental discipline helps you avoid constantly saying no to a child. No one wants to hear that all day, so discipline must be creative and preventive. However, sometimes you cannot protect the child and your valuables in this way, and you have to say no.

I have a good friend who is a skilled musician. She had a rack full of very expensive sheet music, and her one-year-old son discovered that music. He loved the bright colors on the covers and would grab then and chew on them. Obviously, that was expensive material for chewing and really not very healthy for the child. My friend could simply have put the rack on a high shelf so that the child could not reach it. But she knew that there would always be music available, so she blocked out an afternoon of time to teach her son to leave the music alone. These are the steps that she took, and I think you will find this will work for you, as well, if you follow up faithfully.

She explained briefly to the child that he could not have the music. She used the word *no* frequently and firmly. When the child began to reach for the music, she moved him away from it and put the music back in the rack. Clearly and firmly she said, "No, you may not have this." She would pull back the child's hand and not allow him to touch it. She repeated this process with firmness and consistency, until finally, after an hour or two, the child understood that he could not have the music. The lesson had to be repeated each day for several days, but the child was well on his way to learning not to touch the music. And he also learned another very important lesson, that when Mother says no, she means it and will follow through.

Parents sometimes ask if it's necessary to swat or spank a little child. I think that's not necessary, though some argue that a firm swat may be less painful than the consequence of a child's touching a hot iron or a stove.

Keep the time you have with your child full of love,

laughter, and play, and as you and he strengthen the bonds of love, he will become more compliant to please the parent he loves.

TODDLER SIBLING RIVALRY

My question is about disciplining a two year old. How can I guide his behavior to be more kind to his one-year-old sister? They are seventeen months apart. If our son thinks we are not watching, he'll kick her, push her, or hit her with a toy.

I have known older children to seriously hurt a younger sibling. And parents' usual temptation is to protect the child that is picked upon. Actually, the more aggressive, older child is the one that often needs the attention.

Two year olds simply cannot be trusted to play satisfactorily with younger siblings. They usually can't even play successfully with children their own age. They are not really developed enough to do that. They are so busy establishing their own rights and their own identities that they can't cope with the competition of a younger child. This older child desires more time and more attention, especially when he envies the spotlight shining on his younger sister. Don't be afraid to give too much attention to your older child. The parents' attitude in this case needs to become more loving and relaxed, and less worried and critical, and soon the older child will settle down. Parents should, however, provide extra supervision of the toddler until he outgrows his resentment of the baby.

As your son matures, you can try to teach him how to interact with the baby. Help him to hold her for a minute, show him how to stroke her cheeks and help her to grasp his finger. As he discovers the joy of this living "doll," chances are he will stop being rough and learn to be gentle and loving.

IMAGINARY FRIENDS

Should parents be concerned when a small child starts to make up imaginary playmates?

Not at all. In fact, I worry a little when children don't have an imagination that creates playmates and all sorts of fantasies for their little lives. It's quite normal for three- to seven-year-old children to have a great many imaginary friends and even pets. That's part of the creativity of their healthy little minds. Imagining tea parties and creating great banquets from them is something that I can recall from my childhood—along with making mud pies into artistic creations of grandeur and building architectural wonders of string and sticks.

All children have their own various themes of creativity that relate to imagination. You need to enjoy your children's imaginary friends and pets. Enter into that play with them and your own lives will be enriched by their imagination, and theirs, in turn, will be enhanced by your contributions to that sort of play.

Make it clear, however, that both you and your child know that these creatures are imaginary. The only concern that I have is over vagueness that can exist between the imaginary and the real. When children do not know that difference and where that line exists, then I become a little concerned about their being too involved in a fantasy world. By simple words you can help them remember that this is a pretend or imaginary or make-believe situation. A simple verbal indicator can keep both you and your child clear about what is real.

DOING IT THEMSELVES

Why is it so important for a child to be moving toward independence?

There are two reasons. One is for the parents' sake and the other, of course, is for the child's. Parents who tend to take the easy route to keeping a child dependent and overprotected can actually stunt the child's development. It may be easier—or they may enjoy doing everything for him—but it is not good for the child. Children are eventually going to become independent. That's what they're born to do, and that is right for them. It is a natural, gradual process, and the earlier on in the child's life the parents understand that, and work with it, the better both will be.

If parents miss the child's instinctive cues that she is ready for the next stage of development, then it becomes much harder to make that happen later on. For example, a child of three or four wants to help Mommy in the garden or help Daddy do the laundry. But believe me, at thirteen and fourteen that child really will not want to do those things. So teach her to help early on and make that experience a happy and pleasurable one. You will establish good habits of cooperation and will create a sense of responsibility in her. Most rebelliousness in the teenage years can be prevented by knowing how to encourage the gradual establishment of independence and responsibility early in a child's life.

Here are some rules by which you might help yourself and your child in that development. First, *watch the child's interests and capabilities as they develop,* and encourage those abilities early. Such a simple thing as the coordination it takes to hold a glass or the child's feeding herself with a spoon encourages her neurological development. It also helps her feel proud of her independence. Second, *show pride in the child's accomplishments.* Not only does this teach and motivate your child, creating healthy independence, but it also builds the self-esteem she needs. An example: "Susie, how nicely you dressed yourself. What a help that was to me when I was so busy." Not: "Susie, let me do it. You have that shirt on backwards." As painful as it is, and as much extra time and patience as it takes, let the child do it herself. Third, *allow your child to suffer the natural consequences of not doing something right.* Experience is the best teacher, and kids can feel pride when they learn by doing, even if they learn by making a mistake and correcting it.

SHARING AMONG PRESCHOOLERS

Is it possible for two- or three-year-old children to play together and share their toys?

Let's break that down into the two-year-old and the three-year-old, because there is a remarkable difference even in that age span. The typical two year old is truly incapable of interacting in play with other children. The behavior of two year olds really is not very social but quite personal. The two year old is testing his own strength and finding out what he can and cannot do. He is competing with everyone, and the motto of every two year old is "May the better kid win." He needs to find out who is better and stronger.

There are times when kids need that strength, and times when they need to give in. It is important that we not rush our two year olds into social situations that are truly beyond their abilities, and we ought not to demand that they do what they cannot do. Two year olds cannot share, because they don't even know what to do with toys themselves. They need the time and the space to learn that. Require the two year old to stop hurting other children and do not allow him to grab things away from others. Your gentle but firm intervention when your child is around other youngsters will be helpful for protection and guidance for the future. Gradually teach the child how to share and take turns, so that he can learn to play with others successfully later on.

One of the things that two year olds can do very well (and which can help them to learn a great deal about cooperation) is to sit down on the floor and roll a ball back and forth. As you sit down and the child does too, the child will develop a good concept of playing together. That can be an important step in learning cooperation.

Another method for teaching a two year old how to play with others is by putting a number of objects together in a container. You as an adult may play with him by putting things in and taking things out of that container. Then invite another child to do the same thing so that he is doing it with someone his own age. These simple mechanisms can help a two year old to learn how to play with other little people.

Magically, about the age of three, a child will want to play with other children. By then, children have often learned how to share, how to cooperate in all kinds of activities, and how to play imaginatively and creatively together. You will enjoy your three year old's playing with other youngsters.

IN PARENTS' BED

I'd like to find out what your views are on a preschooler coming into bed with his parents during the night. My four year old has been doing this for more than two years. We thought he would tire and stop on his own. He has been a sick child. He doesn't require much sleep and slept through the night for the first time at fifteen months. What can I do to keep him in his own bed, while letting him feel secure and not rejected?

That is a very special question and it addresses two different issues. One is a general philosophy about preschoolers sleeping with parents, and the other is a special child who has had some medical problems.

I am well aware that some authorities believe it is quite okay to allow children to sleep with parents. But generally speaking, I am against this. I think neither parents nor child get adequate rest, and it invades the privacy of the marriage. However, there are times when children are frightened, or when they have been ill, when there are special needs. In the case of illness, I suggest that parents check with a physician to be sure that the child is perfectly all right—that it will be safe for him to sleep in his own bed in his own room. Then, you might try putting his bed temporarily in your bedroom, so he can be nearby without being with you.

When you are ready to break a child of the habit of sleeping with you, be sure that you both are committed to this. You need to be convinced that you are ready for this, and that it will not hurt the child, because it will be difficult to break the habit. When you are convinced, explain to your child what is going to happen. Explain to him why things need to change, including your need for privacy and his need to become more independent. Then establish a ritual for putting him to bed at night. Play with him, quietly rock him, sing to him, read to him, or soothe him in whatever way is comfortable for you and then firmly and lovingly put him in his bed and assure him that he must stay there.

The first night he will test you. I can promise you he will cry, struggle, and use all kinds of devices to make you give in. Hold firm. Do not give in. The second night he will do it a little less, and by the third or fourth night, almost all children will give up the struggle and, frankly, will be relieved to have their own privacy and the spaciousness of their own beds. I know that parents are much more comfortable without that little wiggler between them. Whatever you do, *do not relent.* Simply be consistent and loving.

SHY CHILD

My little girl is three and a half, and I'm sure she is a bright child. She learns things quickly, like a song or a poem, in less than a day. She knows some of her books by heart and can also write part of her name. What worries me is how she responds to other people. If they talk to her, she will hide her face and not answer. She also won't let anyone kiss or hug her except me and sometimes her two sisters. Is there anything I should be doing for her?

One of the much-studied, inborn traits of personality is that of the ability to approach or withdraw from new situations or people. Many a child has been labeled *shy* who is simply inclined to stand back and carefully assess a new situation or person. (Stella Chess, M.D., and Alexander Thomas, M.D., refer to this as the "slow to warm up" child.) Anxious adults tend to push such children socially, thereby creating power struggles which further complicate things.

This is what a shy child needs:

- Parents who accept her unconditionally and do not try to make her something she is not.

- Parents who allow the child to choose to approach other persons, rather than pushing her toward them.

- Parents who give her less attention for performing and more reinforcement for being a child.

I suggest that when you catch your daughter smiling or responding, quietly and enthusiastically compliment her. Try to find some playmates her age and encourage her just to relax.

As you yourself relax, I think you will find that this child will grow to be a loving, warm person.

HAIR PULLING/NAIL BITING

I want to ask you about my son, age two and a half. He has a bad habit of pulling out his hair, especially around bedtime when he is sleepy. He also bites his fingernails. (I do, too.)

If you run your hand over your hair, you find a soft texture that is rather enjoyable. It is not uncommon for children to like to stroke their own hair, or that of their mother, while they are being rocked to sleep as little babies. Pulling out the hair usually begins in an attempt to keep that hair in his hand without having to raise his arm up while he strokes his hair.

I suggest this for this little boy: Provide him with a soft stuffed toy that he can hold when he is sleepy and while you rock him. At this point in his life he may need a little cuddling and babying. Give him something that is silky and pleasing to hold while he falls off to sleep, and perhaps he won't need to pull out his hair. If he tends to eat his hair after pulling it out, I suggest that you not let him, because it will tend to accumulate in his stomach. Hair is not easily digested, and it can create a problem that could require medical attention or even surgery.

Nail biting is another common problem, and one that is not serious but annoying. On a practical basis, nail biting almost always begins because of rough, uneven fingernails that cause discomfort. As the child bites off those rough edges, he may develop a nervous habit that can become a lifelong habit that is hard to break. The solution for nail biting in little children is to keep the nails smooth with a tiny pair of scissors or clippers or a very fine file. I would rub a bit of cream or lotion around the nail bed and the fingernails to prevent hangnails and rough skin. Clear nail polish keeps the nails smooth. It may break the child's habit by giving a different feel to the nails. Also give plenty of physical cuddling and attention to draw the child's focus outward from himself to his environment. I think you will find that those habits eventually will come to a halt.

Some children are born with greater intensity. If your child pulls his hair or bites his nails when he is upset, you will need to teach him to cope differently. Teach him words to describe what he feels, and help him discover what he needs. If he's tired, he may need to be comforted and rocked. If he's angry, help him to express it verbally or by physical exertion that won't harm anyone or anything. Pounding a peg board, for example, can release pent-up frustration.

FIRST-NAME BASIS

I personally prefer to have my young child call me Mommy and her father Daddy, or something indicating we're her parents. But my husband is the director of a camp where all the young people refer to him by his first name. Lately I've noticed that my five year old is picking this up, and I'm concerned about it. Should we avoid a first-name basis with our children? Will it eventually make a difference in our relationship?

Certainly names are important, and so are titles. What does it mean when a child begins to be on a first-name basis with her parents? In fact, what does a first-name basis imply in any relationship?

First, it may imply that we're good friends and that we are equals; or, second, it may imply a lack of respect. Children certainly deserve respect, and they won't learn to show respect unless they are treated with respect. But they are and need to be under parental authority. So one of the expressions of respect is the title by which a child addresses that authority person. I strongly recommend that children call their parents by the titles of Mother and Father, or Mom and Dad. I cannot, however, deny that the basic respect a child shows for the parent is earned, and it is expressed in attitudes and feelings more than titles. So I understand parents who choose to allow their children to call them by their first names. Some parents do that, and frankly, seem to enjoy it. Other parents are so rigid and irritable about demanding a certain title that they lose the affection and the respect they seek.

Chances are this is only a passing phase, but if you decide your child should address you as Mommy and Daddy, simply explain that she is different from the campers. Because your relationship with her is so important, you want to be called by a special name that only you and your children share.

PUBLIC TANTRUMS

What can we do when our three-year-old son throws a loud temper tantrum in public? His favorite trick is to throw himself down and scream over some little thing in a store or restaurant. He doesn't seem to respond to threats of what will happen when we get home, but we also have hesitated to spank him in front of people.

That is a difficult situation. Children commonly have temper tantrums. They begin at about eighteen to twenty-four months of age and may extend into the early grade-school years. Most children begin having tantrums out of frustration. They simply reach the end of their resources, and in angry desperation they throw themselves down and cry and kick. That gets their anger out, but it usually arouses the anger of parents. Unfortunately, with those early tantrums children may gain certain benefits, and they learn to have fits in order to get their way. It sounds as if that's what this child is doing. By kicking and screaming, he knows he can embarrass his parents and get whatever he wants.

Knowing that helps you understand how to deal with his tantrums. First of all, make it clear to your child (and at two or three years of age, certainly the child will understand what you say) that he will not have any more temper tantrums in public. Explain this *before* you go anywhere at all. Tell your child that you will not tolerate his fits, and decide carefully what you will do. For example, you could decide that if your child throws a fit, you will leave the store immediately and take him home. That usually is quite a punishment because children like going to stores and enjoy the excitement of being with their parents. You may decide, on the other hand, that a time-out would help. The time-out refers to a short period of time (often one minute for each year of age) spent in a spot designated by the parent. This may mean taking him to the car and giving him a three-minute time-out in his car seat, or just sitting him down in a corner of the store for that period of time. Leaving him home with your spouse or a sitter the next time may be another consequence that will help him decide to change. Whatever you decide, be sure to follow through. Children are quick to detect if this is an idle threat or if you really mean business.

Often children simply are not mature enough to handle themselves well in public, and if your child is not ready for such privileges, don't hesitate to get a baby sitter and leave him at home. Above all, do not allow your child's fits to gain him any advantages *ever*. You will be glad that you were firm, and that you went through the inconveniences, when your child finally gives up throwing fits.

WETTING PROBLEM

I'm asking about my son who is four and a half

years old. He wets the bed at night if I don't get him up, and then sometimes he still wets. He even wets all through the day unless I constantly remind him to use the bathroom. He will say he doesn't have to go, and then in the next few minutes, he's wet. It doesn't seem to bother him. He never asks to be changed. I've talked to his doctor, and he thinks my son is just lazy. I haven't taken him to any specialists.

In this case I would recommend that the mother seek the advice of a specialist, because at four and a half a child who habitually wets may have some special problems (though that is rare). Often wetting is not a physical problem but an emotional one. It may be due to worrisome events in the life of the child. The arrival of a new baby, a move, illness among relatives—all of these events can cause fear, guilt, and anger, a dangerous triad in a child's life. These can cause him to regress and to wet his pants again, even when he has been well trained. Let me say emphatically that this does not mean that it is the parents' fault if the child wets. But parents can help find the solution by understanding the problem and trying these suggestions.

Conflict between the child and his parents is one cause of both bed-wetting and daytime wetting. Another cause (and I suspect it in the case of this child) is that a child is so busy and involved in play that he doesn't take the time to go to the bathroom. *He* doesn't mind being wet and why should his mother?

There are numerous cures for bed-wetting. There is an alarm device that can be ordered from a catalog. This goes off at the first drops of moisture, as the child begins to wet, and by awakening the child can condition him to wake up before wetting the bed; then he can go to the bathroom. However, this is a drastic and rather negative solution, as it is quite disturbing to a child to be suddenly awakened from a sound sleep by this alarm.

Sometimes when children are a bit older and still wetting their pants, the parents may need to put them back in diapers for a while. I recommend that you do this sensitively, without shaming the child, and let him know that when he is ready to use the bathroom, he can stop wearing the diapers. (The type of diapers that can be pulled down to use the toilet are perfect for this problem, as a child can wear them without feeling ashamed.) Be sure that you are not nagging or fussing at the child. Simply explain to your child the reasons for stopping the wetting: it creates an offensive odor, he will be starting school soon, it makes work for others, etc. Set up a plan with your child, giving him certain privileges that he can earn by staying dry. Set a timer to remind him to go to the bathroom, but do not get into a power struggle if he refuses. Lots of love, encouragement, optimism, and patience will help you and your child through the rigors of toilet training.

WHINING

Within the past few months my four year old has become quite a whiner. When asked to do anything like clean up her room, she stomps her feet and performs what I would call a whining temper tantrum. She also is quite argumentative if I say she can't do something. She pleads, whines, and argues with me. I can't seem to find a way to stop this, short of spanking her or sending her to her room.

Whining is an aggravating habit for most parents. When a child is four and has just become a whiner, I am very curious about what may have caused that to begin. Is there a new baby in the family, perhaps, that makes her want to be a little child again? Is she worried about attending school in the near future? Any major event or threat that can cause the child to feel afraid or insecure and make her want to be younger than she is, can cause whining.

On the other hand, perhaps this child has observed someone else, such as a friend, getting her way by whining. Fits and whining and tantrums all have something in common. They get for a child something that she wants very much.

Here are some suggestions that can help you eliminate this behavior: When both you and the child are calm, explain to her that you will not tolerate whining any longer. Tell her what will happen if she does it again (and be quite clear about that). Be prepared to follow through. I frankly like the idea of sending the child to a time-out chair or to her room rather than spanking. In this kind of temperamental child, a spanking will tend to make her more rebellious instead of helping. Be certain that the child does what you have asked her to do *no matter what.* I occasionally find that parents send a child to the room and the child still does not have to do the task or follow through with the request.

Most whining indicates a child's need to "be little." They need more cuddling, warmth, even babying for a while. Not as a reward for whining, but as a response to a need, offer bits of pampering. It will at some point saturate your child's spirit, and she will stop whining.

Do not let your child's anger or whining influence you. Do not let that habit make you give in, because it will only create a firmer habit and a stronger sense of power in the child.

You might find it helps to work *with* your child to clean her room. Children this age really do not understand what we mean when we say, "clean your room." Instead, have her help you with jobs; working together can be fun. Changing beds can be a great game. Teach your child to express her feelings verbally, but require responsibility in spite of how she feels. And praise her when she succeeds.

PEER PRESSURE

I have a four-and-a-half-year-old son who is easily led by other children. Even if he knows he shouldn't do something, he does it anyway, because, he says, "They wanted me to," or "They asked me to." How can I help him to think and act on his own?

That's an important question, and the timing is crucial. We usually think of peer pressure as a problem that only teenagers face. In fact, however, even very young children can feel these same pressures to conform and act as their friends do. I find that parents sometimes are successful in teaching obedience to their child, but in teaching obedience they have forgotten to think about the need for teaching good judgment and for developing the child's individuality. In addition, there are some children who are simply very adaptive. They are compliant and tend to follow the crowd.

With a child of this type, *commend your child for his willingness to obey.* He needs to feel good about himself, and this is certainly a good characteristic. After you have explained that good quality about him, *describe the need to take another step in his thinking and development.* The child needs to consider whom he is to obey—and what he is doing when he obeys someone else. Even young children, for example, understand what it means to inflict damage or pain on another child, so use that knowledge with him. Help him know what is okay to do (things that are creative and positive), and what is not okay to do (things that are damaging or painful to himself, someone else, or someone else's property). Is a friend or playmate asking him to do something that is likely to hurt someone else? Will this action make your son feel badly about himself later on? Would he be ashamed or sad if you found out he did it? If someone else did this to him, would he feel badly?

These concepts can be taught even to a young child and can help him develop compassion and empathy and help him become a fine adult.

Giving the child some weeks to work on these questions is also important. He certainly has to have discipline and supervision if he is to live out the answers that you are trying to teach him. Remember, parents, being a leader is not too important. We need only a few. But being an individual, strong enough to take a stand for what is right—and wise enough to know what is right—is the essence of good character. Help your child develop it.

LEAVING A CHILD IN NURSERY

How do you leave a child in a church nursery? We've tried, and we've already done everything wrong. First, we kept our daughter out of the nursery until she was about a year and a half because she always cried there. Then when we did decide to leave her, we made the mistake of sneaking out. She really threw a fit when she realized we were gone. Now it's really a problem.

That's a common problem, and I spent a number of months working in my own church's nursery, so I understand the other side of that difficulty as well. I have a plan that I have found works a great many times, and I would like to suggest it. You will need to plan to miss the church service for a couple of weeks. You may alternate that between you, as mother and father, but this is what I suggest that you do. (With variations, this works in a nursery or any other childcare facility.)

First, explain to your two year old, who will understand a good deal more than you might think, that you are not going to feel sorry for her when she stays in the nursery, that you know it will be good for her to learn to play with other children and to give you the freedom to attend the church. Whatever your explanation, make it very clear—you are *not* giving her a choice but explaining your decision.

On the other hand, let her know that you certainly understand her fear of the strangeness and that she will miss you and want to be with you. Now when you go to church with her the next time (after you have given this ceremonious explanation to your child), take her with you to the sanctuary. Let her see where you will be sitting and then walk with her from the sanctuary to the nursery. Knowing the exact route will give her a little more security.

When you place her in the nursery, do not act ambivalent. If you are unsure about leaving her, she will pick up on that and will be unsure herself. Leave her the first time (after your talk) for as short a time as two minutes. Leave her, telling her that you will be back in a very short time. Then return to her promptly, so that she knows you will follow through and that you will be back. The next time you leave, make it five minutes, and gradually increase the time that you are away. Consistently returning to her will help her to know that she is not abandoned, that you *will* be back, and that you are reliable parents.

You will, of course, need to make the nursery supervisors aware of your plan so they can cooperate with you. I suspect they will be more than glad to have such a plan working, rather than to have a screaming child for an hour every Sunday. The following week, I recommend that again you go through this leaving and returning process. Within three or four Sundays, I can almost guarantee that you will find that your child will be staying in the nursery happily playing away, and you may attend church with absolute peace of mind.

3

SCHOOL-AGE CHILDREN

SUMMER CAMP?

Many of us have wonderful memories of attending summer camp, but watching your child wave goodbye from the window of a moving bus is a terrible experience. Will my child be homesick? Will he be sent home with poison ivy or broken bones? Will he be able to get to sleep without a bedtime story? Is camp a good experience for children?

I think summer camp is a wonderful experience for children, but it does need some good judgment and planning. Usually camp is something good, but there are children who suffer severe attacks of homesickness and have difficulty adjusting to the large numbers of children, the scheduled activities, and the new adults that supervise them. In order to find out if your child is really ready for summer camp, here are some questions that may help you:

Is your child ready to go? Because all of the other kids of a similar age are going off with excitement does not mean that your child is ready. Be careful to ask that question honestly, without overprotecting and without pushing your child to go. By the age of nine or ten, almost all children can go to camp for a week, and they will really enjoy it. That doesn't mean that *every* child is ready by that age.

Has the child had a previous unpleasant experience being away overnight? If an overnight visit with a friend has been an unpleasant or frightening experience, the child may still have some fear that could make going away difficult.

Is the child afraid that you want to be rid of him? Does he think you will give extra attention to a brother or sister while he is away from you? Find out the camp's policy regarding phone calls home or parental visits if the child becomes a little homesick. Some camps are lenient, and others are very strict. If the child can call home, be positive and reassuring, rather than sympathetic and rescuing.

What is the camp program? Does it offer activities that your child really likes and is good at? Or does it emphasize areas of life that your child doesn't particularly care about? If you have a lurking fear that camp this year may not be good for your child, do not hesitate to wait. There's always another year, and perhaps next year will be a far better time.

BABY TALK

My eleven-year-old granddaughter talks baby talk to get attention. Isn't she a bit old to be acting like this? She's the oldest of four children, and the apple of Daddy's eye. She often tattles to get her brothers into trouble with their parents. I'd appreciate some help in how to handle this situation and yet keep a good relationship with everyone.

That certainly is a sensitive situation, and I would recommend that this grandmother work hard to comment on the good qualities about this granddaughter, both to the child and to her parents. She needs to make some comments that show how much she loves and enjoys the child before she gets into the problem areas. I suggest that Grandmother wait until the problem becomes so explicit that it can't be explained away or denied. After the episode is over (the tattling, or the manipulating of her father, or whatever that particular episode might be), then that grandmother should wait for a quiet time alone with the parent with whom she can be most open. She can then discuss with that parent her concerns about the child and those particular problem areas. However, just the concern alone is not very helpful, so I would suggest that the grandmother give them some constructive advice.

Oldest children, unfortunately, have to grow up too soon, and they usually feel displaced by younger brothers and sisters. They sometimes need babying of sorts, and this child's tendency to talk baby talk reflects her need to be treated as a little child now and then. Staying little or reverting to being little from time to time is something that perhaps all of us crave. The parents should understand that need of the older daughter, and give her a little bit of extra affection and attention, alone and away from those younger brothers.

She particularly may need some special time with Mom. I find that a girl who is strictly Daddy's girl often craves time with Mother, but somehow doesn't feel as though she can get it. This mother may want to spend a little more time alone with this girl and give her some special mother/daughter attention. Dad and Mother, in this case, may need to reverse their roles a little bit. It sounds like the father has been the nurturer for this child, and at this point the mother, I think, should take over the role. Let Dad become a little bit more the disciplinarian.

Grandmother unfortunately can only go so far, and I would recommend to this grandmother a practice that I follow myself. That is, that she make suggestions, offer advice, particularly offer her love, and then let go. Trust your child and his or her spouse to do a good job as parents. Simply love their child and trust them to do the same kind of job with their children that you did with them.

AFTER-SCHOOL ACTIVITIES

I suppose that many parents who work away from home would be interested in your opinion about how much supervision a ten year old might need during the time between the end of school and when his parents get home from work. Do I need to get a baby sitter (which my son doesn't want)? Or can he manage on his own?

Before I answer that specifically, I would like to share a story of an actual case that I worked with. One of the schools in which I used to consult was having a major problem with a fifth-grade child. He was getting into a great deal of trouble at school, and children were coming to school and reporting problems that he created in the neighborhood. When we called his mother to come in and talk with us, she was indignant and assured us that it couldn't possibly be true that her son was behaving badly after school. She told me that she always insisted that her son telephone her as soon as he got home, and in talking with him she was convinced that he was just fine. What she did not realize, of course, was that after the son made his call, he was going out and creating trouble.

A child of ten or eleven cannot be assumed to be able to get along just fine without you. If possible, I recommend that one of the parents be home within a few minutes of the child's arrival. If it is impossible, here are some suggestions that can help you decide what to do in providing the proper supervision and protection for your children.

Evaluate your neighborhood. Know who lives next door to you and even around the block. Is yours a reasonably safe community in which children can play together outside with the supervision of other neighborhood parents? Are there children who could influence your child to get into trouble, or who would be ready partners in mischief your own child created? Are your neighbors friendly? Are they at home much of the time, and would they be available in case there was an emergency or some need?

Evaluate your child. Is your son truly responsible and honest, or is he, as most children are, capable of being deceptive when he thinks you don't know about it? Is he easily tempted to mischief, or is he a responsible child with plenty of things to do after school (such as homework, practicing an instrument, or using a computer)? If he uses a computer, will he avoid the many damaging opportunities on the Internet?

Evaluate your job. Does it allow you and your child to contact each other if needed in case of a problem? Would you be able to leave on the spur of the moment if necessary?

If several of the above conditions are such that you feel concern for his safety, your child will have to bow to your good judgment and accept a sitter. Don't overprotect your child, but do protect him enough to keep him safe. Fortunately, more and more schools are adding before- and after-school care to their programs, and many community agencies also sponsor child-care for older kids that is more geared to their interests.

UNDESIRABLE FRIENDS

I'm upset about our twin boys, eleven years old, copying their friends. One boy's friend is nice but hyper and picks his food apart like a monkey. My son gets angry at me when I ask him not to act like his friend. My other boy's friend is being raised by

his grandparents and is spoiled and rebellious. I just don't understand why my sons can't be themselves.

Friends are a very important part of a child's life, and interestingly, children need their parents' approval of their friends much more than their disapproval. Look at the positive aspects of your children's friends and comment on those. The children themselves will pick up the defects and the negative aspects of those kids in time.

Welcome the friends into your home, but be around to observe. Of course you need to make your rules very clear. Do this without embarrassing your child or estranging your child's friends. Help your children to see the wonderful qualities of their friends and learn to emulate those qualities, but also help them to understand their faults and avoid them.

Having imperfect friends allows great opportunities to compliment your own children for the areas of their lives in which they shine. Teach your children to help their friends become better people. In doing that they will learn to feel better about themselves and you.

CHILDREN WHO FIGHT

Why do some children constantly get into fights?

There are a number of reasons:

1. Some family philosophies communicate to kids that it's smart to be aggressive. If you believe as a parent that you have to fight to get along in this world, then you may be teaching your children to become so aggressive that they can get into social problems.

2. Another reason children fight is that they feel put down or inferior to other children, particularly siblings. A child who

does not get enough positive strokes or loving attention may learn to fight and act aggressively, preferring punishment or scolding to no attention at all. When such behavior is encouraged by the family situation, it will carry over to those outside the family as well.

3. Other children react angrily to fear and insecurity. Perhaps the typical school bully is the example that we're all familiar with. The bully is a child who is, underneath it all, very insecure and frightened. This child covers it up by pretending to be a tough guy. He gets into fights with other children.

4. Finally, some aggression and fighting is instinctive. There is an inborn need to protect or defend oneself and those who are dear to us. That may be why some children fight.

Look through these reasons and try to understand why it is that your child is a fighter. If your child is fighting because he is afraid, then you need to encourage him to talk out his fear. If he is fighting because he doesn't get enough positive attention, then give that to him to help him feel more confident and secure. If, unwittingly, you are teaching your child that you have to be a fighter to get along in this world, then change your approach and teach him how to love as well as to protect himself.

Meanwhile, establish a rule against fighting. Teach your child what to do instead of fighting, for example, discussing and solving problems, seeking adult counsel or intervention, or simply walking away. You can make a positive difference in your community by teaching love and logic instead of allowing aggression.

PREPARING FOR ADOLESCENCE

Since parents can't stop the teenage years from coming, what can they do to get ready?

You really do need to get ready, and *before adolescence* is the time to strengthen your child's personality foundations and prepare her for the onslaught of those difficult teenage years.

1. Remember your own preadolescent years. What was particularly troublesome to you, and what would have helped you (or what *did* help you) to get through those times? Try to watch for those same needs in your teen.

2. Don't forget that adolescents are confused. Many adolescents feel socially inadequate and don't quite know where they fit with one another or with adults. Some days they feel and act twenty-five, and other days they seem to be two!

3. Work hard developing good communication skills. Be careful to listen to your child, as well as to talk with her as you would to a friend. And learn to listen with your heart as well as your ears.

4. Begin to move out of the parenting role. Adolescence is a time when parents are called on to carefully balance the parenting skills that you have developed up to now, and the need to become a friend to your child. Learn how to disagree without being disagreeable. Show respect when she expresses feelings or ideas, even if they sound weird. Be glad she is learning to think for herself and tactfully guide that thinking.

5. Prepare for puberty. Get your preteen ready for the dramatic physical changes of puberty. Many more children now are entering puberty in the fourth and fifth grades. These children are not expecting such early changes, and they can feel quite confused and surprised if they have not been properly educated about these natural changes. So, learn what you must in order to teach your child about the sexual development that he or she will experience and how to understand the opposite sex, as well as themselves.

6. Be wary of the social changes in school. Many kids in the tender years of twelve to fourteen must move from being at the top level in their elementary school to being at the bottom level of junior high or middle school. They will experience

intense peer pressure, and they need you to counter the negative pressure they face.

7. Give them as much freedom as they can safely handle, but as much protection as they need!

4

TEENS

NAME-BRAND CLOTHING

Our thirteen-year-old daughter is our oldest child, and I am concerned about the great amount of peer pressure she feels. There is a lot of pressure from her classmates to dress a certain way and also to achieve. This is hard on her and also on her father and me. Do you have any suggestions about how we can help her?

Yes, I do. That question is one that applies to many, many families today. In fact, I've had mothers of five and six year olds concerned about their children's being taunted because they didn't wear jeans or shoes of a certain brand. In today's economy, few parents can afford those expensive items, and I do not think it is healthy for children to believe that they must have name brands in order to measure up to their friends. Some communities have decided to require uniforms in public schools in order to limit the problems related to clothing fashions (and gangs).

Parents should decide where you will allow your child to be

similar to her peers and where you will set the boundaries and require her to be an individual. When a child is so different that she sticks out in relation to other friends and peers, she can be socially limited. I knew a child once who was not allowed to watch television, go skating, or wear any of the things his friends did, and he felt isolated and strange. On the other extreme, I know parents who sacrifice so much that they almost become enslaved to the whims of society and their children's friends.

Once you as parents have decided on what you can and will allow, then I suggest you include your daughter in a discussion. Listen to and respect her point of view, and then share your ideas with her. Be frank about your reasons for setting limits. This may be just financial stress, or it may entail her need to develop her individuality. Consider giving her a clothing budget that she must live with, and then allow her within that budget to decide what she wants to buy.

Begin a quiet campaign that consistently reflects to your child your value of her special gifts and abilities. In developing these qualities of her being and her character, I hope you will find that she gets such a healthy degree of self-esteem that she will not need those external items to feel good about herself. And you will have prepared her for the teen pressure to come!

REBELLION OR INDEPENDENCE?

How can parents tell if their teenager is rebelling or just trying out a new idea?

There are some very specific guidelines that can help parents to make that differentiation.

Attitude. A truly rebellious teenager almost constantly has a hostile, sarcastic, or cynical attitude. He is secretive over prolonged periods of time and becomes manipulative and tricky. It's hard for the child or parent to really trust one another if he is a rebellious teenager.

Behavior. Not only is the teenager's attitude important, but so is his behavior. The committed rebel is potentially destructive in the things that he does. If not destructive in the sense of physical damage, the rebellious teenager is destructive of himself as a human being. He does things that disqualify him for trust or respect by other people. Rebelliousness also is generalized, and includes rebelling in school by not getting the schoolwork done. There is also rebelling socially by misbehaving, sometimes in serious ways; rebelling at home by not following the rules; refusing to attend church. Across the board there is a resistance to the rules or expectations of the family and society in general.

Resentment. That is another one of the characteristics of rebellious teenagers. As parents examine themselves, I find that many of them discover that they have been too rigid and controlling for too long a time. Extreme control and severe punishment both contribute to resentment.

The child who is going through a healthy search for independence will argue over specific ideas or values or rules. He needs to argue in order to stretch his own growing intellect. He needs to be listened to and argued with, in good humor, in order to develop his self-respect and establish his real beliefs and values. But this child will soon return to his basic goodwill and love for his family. Studies show that parents are the most important influence in a teen's life. So keep your influence positive and strong.

TEEN FINANCES

Our high schooler needs to develop financial responsibility. She has her own bank account, but we buy

**all of her clothes and give her money for school
lunches and other expenses. She works part-time,
and we're wondering what expenses she should contribute to. Also, how can we get her to keep financial records? Should we expect her to budget?**

Once these parents are basically agreed on financial values,
then they can arrange a kind of business meeting with their
daughter. Discuss the following issues openly and frankly, but
kindly and intellectually:

First, what are the daughter's expenses and the family's?
What is the cost of living? What are her future plans? Is she
going away to college, or does she plan on some special job
training? Does she want to buy a car or get her own apartment?
What are the costs of all of these rather major things that
children sometimes want a few years down the road? Discuss
together how she can best prepare herself for those future plans
and what you parents can and cannot do to help.

Next, help her outline a simple budget and then put the
information in an accounting book or on a computer program.
If she is not going to college or into some other special training,
then I think she should begin contributing to the family budget,
saving money, and planning for her future.

If she is mature and responsible, you could put her in charge
of all her own needs. Supplement her income if you need to,
and help her figure out ways to pay for all her clothes, trans-
portation, meals, and so on, from what she receives. Encourage
her to set aside savings and a tithe for church or charity before
other needs.

Keep this positive and helpful, and avoid disapproval or
blame. I think you will find that helping a child manage
money will also teach a great many other values for successful living.

TEENAGE DISCIPLINE

How should parents approach the situation when a teenager has done something that's really wrong?

First, the parents need to *verify the facts.* You will lose your child's respect if you jump to conclusions, assuming he is wrong when perhaps he is not. I will never forget the time we had a call from the police station about our adolescent son and his friend. We were told that they had been caught shoplifting from a local store. But when we went to the police station to check out all of the facts, we discovered that it was a case of mistaken identity. It had not been our son at all.

Second, if you do know that a wrong has been done by your child, *"cool it."* Simply do nothing until you get control of your emotions and can handle the situation with wisdom and caution.

Third, sit down with your child. You, the child, and any other significant people can *discuss the situation* in private. I recommend that you not question the young person if you are certain that he has done the act. Asking him direct questions will often add to the problem by prompting him to lie about it. Review with the child what was wrong with what was done. Be sure that the child understands what he did, why it was wrong, and how it might hurt a number of people as well as himself.

Fourth, *wait for the child* to recognize the wrongdoing and want to make amends. It is one thing for you as parents to know that it's wrong. But it will not help your child to grow in maturity and understanding unless *he* knows what was wrong about it. A friend of mine endured immense grief over a serious act of vandalism by her teenage son. He refused to admit it, but she learned undeniably that he had done it. After much thought, she took a long book to read and went to his room. "Neither of us will leave this room until you have told the truth," she said matter-of-factly. She then sat and began reading her book. Two hours later, her son finally revealed the facts. Together, they worked out a way for him to remedy his act. He was relieved, and learned a lifetime of lessons in a single day!

Fifth, *set up a consequence* that will be meaningful to your child. It should be one that will help her to see the seriousness of the act and to prevent a recurrence of the problem.

Finally, *look for any underlying reasons* for the misbehavior. Perhaps the child had a valid reason for what she did that you were unaware of. Or perhaps she is seeking attention or acting out some worry or anxiety. If serious wrongdoing is repeated frequently, I urge you to seek counsel that will help diagnose and cure such actions.

BIRTH-CONTROL INFORMATION

Would parents who feel very strongly about sexual morality be encouraging their teenagers toward promiscuity by telling them about contraceptives?

That's a question that a great many parents have asked. By the time their children become teenagers, parents should have taught them a sense of morality. By that I mean what makes a particular act right or wrong. They should have given their children a set of values to live by and have taught them how to understand their sexuality and control their impulses, how to be sensitive toward each other, and how to act responsibly in social and dating situations. If that moral teaching has not occurred prior to adolescence, parents will have some work to do very quickly.

Most parents intuitively know when their children are becoming interested in sexual practices—they have reached puberty and are expressing an interest in the opposite sex. If you have not already done so, this is the time to discuss sexual activity with your child. Your child needs to know how he or she is allowed to relate to the opposite sex (e.g., "friendships and group outings are okay, but no actual dating until age fifteen") and why. But don't stop there. Talk to your child specifically about what sexual behaviors you feel should be saved for a later age and what should be saved for marriage. Make it clear, for example by citing research and Scripture, why you feel the way you do about intercourse before marriage. But don't be too negative. Also, teach your teens that sexual intimacy is a beautiful, fun, and even sacred experience. That's a big reason why it should be saved for the person one marries for life.

However, you must also be realistic. If you have raised your child to share your moral values and you have not been overly rigid, then you can be assured that your children will, deep down, have a desire to live up to your expectations. But you must take into account the impulsivity of the typical teen, the pressure for early sexual activity in some social groups, the desire for rebellion in some cases, and even the frequency of date rape. You have to communicate to your children why you have serious concerns about sexual activity. Then I recommend that you also talk to them about pregnancy, sexually transmitted diseases (STDs), and contraception. And be sure to talk to both daughters *and sons* about these issues.

Contraception is a very controversial topic, and there are many in Christian circles who feel that any talk about contraception will encourage sexual activity. But I do not agree. If contraceptive information is given by you, in the context of a strong set of moral values, I believe it will give the child the information needed without encouraging sexual activity. You can stress that the only guaranteed protection against STDs and pregnancy is abstinence. (There are a number of social groups now that encourage abstinence, such as the "True Love Waits" movement.)

Parents, be careful that you not become so rigid that you

push your children in the very direction that you want them to avoid. One of the saddest situations I knew was a young woman from a conservative home who was pregnant out of wedlock. When she explained to me how it was that she had allowed herself to become sexually active, she told me that her mother had been so strict that she simply had to rebel in order to prove to her mother "that she can't boss everything I do."

On the other hand, you should not be so "laid-back" that you fail to make your moral values clear and fail to give your teen the information he or she needs to make informed decisions. Providing no information is as bad as giving a child the wrong information. They both lead to poor decision making.

If you believe your teen is sexually active, I suggest that you thoughtfully and prayerfully sit down with your teenager. If you have a healthy, open, and affirming relationship, you can ask why he or she is becoming sexually involved. Does she know what needs are being fulfilled? Has he been under strong pressure from peers? Is there a fear that she might lose her boyfriend if she does not go along with him? Does he feel his girlfriend expects him to make advances? Have there been parties with alcohol or other drugs and a high level of sexual overtones? Try to help your adolescent understand and try to understand what he or she is dealing with. Perhaps you can help your teen get needs met in a more wholesome way. In fact, teach your teens how to plan such fun activities with friends that they won't think about having sex. Also teach them to recognize sexual arousal and to set boundaries to control it.

If, on the other hand, you do not have the kind of open relationship that would allow such a discussion to take place, then you are in a much more difficult position and probably have little influence on your child's behavior. If your teen is sexually active, get him or her as much information as possible about contraception and protection. Be sure to include both subjects, as many forms of contraception do nothing to protect someone from a sexually transmitted disease. Offer to take your rebellious child to the doctor or a clinic, pay for the visit, and foot the bill for contraception and protection. If you can do this calmly, while still making your own moral position clear, it may be the beginning of a return to a more open relationship between you. And, as always, pray for guidance for yourself and a change of heart for your child. ("True Love Waits" even has a specialized program for those who have been sexually active but want to be abstinent again.)

UNDERSTANDING TEENAGE PREGNANCY

From your experience with pregnant teenagers, what would you say a girl in this situation needs most from her parents?

Interestingly, one of the most important aids that a pregnant girl seems to need is the help and support of her father. She needs her mother, but during this time somehow dads are especially important. In working with a great many teenage pregnancies, I found one of the common denominators of them was an emotional distance from their fathers. In fact, many studies indicate that estrangement from her father is a major factor in becoming intimate with a man. So, Dad, you need to spend time with that daughter, even though it's a sensitive time in her life. This can give her a chance to understand herself and her relationship with her boyfriend, because many times that boyfriend is symbolic of you as the dad. Many children (and so often they are really children at heart) do not know why they become sexually involved or how it was that they allowed themselves to become so irresponsible. Here are some points that you need to understand in this regard.

Many times young people's involvement in sexual activity comes from their need for *someone to love* them—someone to prove to them that they are desirable and someone to belong to. Other young people are trying to *prove their sexuality.* Women may have a need to feel feminine, and their boyfriends to feel masculine. Some young people even desire to become pregnant. They think that having a child will give them someone to love and *be loved by.* The desire to gain *attention* from their parents and especially from fathers is a major subconscious (and perhaps even a conscious) part of the needs of these young people. Searching for tangible evidence of love is a common denominator in the young people who become sexually active.

From these needs and inner feelings of teenagers, you can see that what daughters need most from you is love, acceptance, forgiveness, the security of your definite commitment to them, and the will to make sense out of a difficult situation while growing in responsibility.

TEEN PREGNANCY: THE PRACTICAL ISSUES

What steps would you recommend that parents take when they find out their unmarried daughter is pregnant?

First, the parents need to get their daughter to a doctor. A physician must confirm the diagnosis of the pregnancy, being sure that the mother's state of health and that of her unborn child are the very best they can be. The mother will want to know when the baby is likely to be born and what preparations must be made prior to that time.

Second, I strongly recommend that the family go together (at least the parents and the daughter, perhaps the father and his parents as well) to a counselor who is skilled in such issues. Making choices about this child and its imminent birth is something that very few people can do well alone because of the many emotional factors involved. Sometimes seeing a pastor or priest is helpful, especially because many young men and women feel guilty about their irresponsibility and the hurt they have caused their parents.

The choices that are available:

Marriage is possible in many cases, though not all. Marriage is not something to be undertaken lightly. If having sex outside marriage was wrong, marrying someone with whom one might be incompatible will not make it right. Further, 70 to 80 percent of teen marriages end up in divorce in less than five years.

Keeping the baby and raising it is another option that demands a great deal of help from those supportive of the mother. Parents must be honest about whether they can conscientiously offer that choice to their daughter, since much of the burden may fall on them.

Adoption is a third choice, and for many young women this is the wisest but most immediately painful solution. This can be done through a qualified agency which can look for a stable family to raise the child.

Abortion is one of the choices your child will probably be offered, though you may try to prevent its being offered. I strongly recommend that parents encourage their daughter to not choose that avenue. Talk with the clergy. Speak with a Christian counselor. Take enough time to think carefully about this, because the aftermath of abortion is often fraught with serious guilt and depression over the death of this child, along with possible medical complications.

Be wise. Take enough time to make your decision carefully and consider the future of your child and yourself. Be prayerful, and I know that you will make the best decision that you can make.

TEENAGE PREGNANCY AND PARENTS' FEELINGS

How should parents deal with their feelings when they discover their teenager is pregnant?

My experience with both parents and young women who are pregnant out of wedlock has been tragically extensive. At first parents go through all the stages of grief. They want to deny that this has ever happened. Shock and denial are almost always followed by anger. "Why did you do this to me?" or "How *could* you?" are common verbal responses.

Then there comes a preoccupation, a sadness, a real depression. Often there is guilt. ("I have failed. . . ." "I've been a bad parent.") They may blame each other, or the school, or the boy. There are all kinds of very strong negative reactions that parents experience in this crisis. But let me reassure you that you *will* recover from all these painful feelings, and eventually you can be restored to peace of mind and joy in living.

How can you cope with these strong feelings? Express them in words to one another, to your physician, perhaps your pastor, or a trusted friend. The more you can talk about the sadness, the pain, the worry, the anger, the more quickly you will recover from the intensity of those feelings. Above all, let your daughter know that despite the pain that this event causes, you still love her. Never allow her to think, even for a minute, that you will abandon her or fail to help her through this time.

Get good counseling for yourself and her, and, of course, good medical attention for this mother-to-be. Listen to your child without condemning her or judging her. You will need to make some very important decisions in the days ahead about who will raise the baby, and you will need to work together to make these decisions wisely. If you are to get through these months with positive problem solving, you must find wisdom, patience, and unconditional acceptance of your child. She, in turn, needs to learn a sense of mature responsibility and good judgment.

Also, parents, don't forget your responsibility if your son is the father of a baby conceived out of wedlock. Your feelings will be very similar to those of the teen mother, but your son's needs will differ. He needs to face up to his responsibility for the financial and emotional needs of this child. Even if he will not marry the mother, he should remain involved with the child if it is not given up for adoption. And he also needs to know that you will stand by him and continue to love him in spite of this large mistake he has made.

COLLEGE?

How can parents and young people decide if college is the right move?

A decade ago I would have had no difficulty answering that question glibly. "Of course, *all* young people should go to college." With increasing college costs, however, this simply is not reasonable for everyone. And there are options for education through various means, such as trade schools, that do not require four years of college. I will offer you some guidelines that can help parents know how to advise their children.

One is the student's own *motivation.* When that young person has studied conscientiously and has reasonably good grades, has an interest in going on to college and learning the kinds of material that colleges present, then that person should have an opportunity to explore more advanced schooling. Even those with poor grades in high school can succeed in college if their desire is intense.

The second guideline is the teachers' and counselors' recommendations regarding your child's *academic capabilities.* Speak with them and take their advice as to whether your child is likely to be successful in college at this time.

Special vocational testing and guidance can give you additional help in knowing whether your child's abilities lie in academic pursuits or in those of some other occupation. Check with a high-school counselor or the career program at a local community college to see what sorts of testing is available, what it will cost, and whether a career counselor might help a child to see his or her options for future work. If your child's gifts are not academic, but more along the lines of learning by doing and working with the hands, you might want to encourage him or her to look into apprenticeships for learning a trade. Various careers, such as the construction trades and the food industry, offer apprenticeships. Your focus ought to be on honing your child's skills, whatever these are.

A third guideline may be the very practical consideration of your *ability to afford* to send your child to college or your child's ability to earn enough for school. Loans and grants are not always available. Helping to earn their own expenses is, of course, still an option for young people, as is attending less expensive, local colleges for the first two years of schooling.

Some young people need to take a job for a while before attending college. This is risky, and the child may become so addicted to the paycheck that she may not want to leave it. On the other hand, jobs can become so boring and monotonous that students will realize they want more education, and then they can go off to college with greater motivation. Also, some colleges (more and more all the time) have work/study options that allow students to take time off to work in their chosen fields. This can be an excellent way of testing out the career and making personal contacts with future employers.

Community or junior college is a wonderful opportunity that is not very costly and allows the young person to have a little more time at home to grow up and to know what he or she really wants to do. State colleges and universities generally are less expensive than private schools. Church-related or Christian colleges offer spiritual training and development for young people and should be considered an option if your finances allow for a private school.

AMBITIOUS TEENAGER

> **My high schooler loves to be a part of everything (class officer, school play, athletics, and more). He does carry responsibility well, but I'm wondering if I should help him say no. How many extra activities are good for a teenager?**

Perhaps I can answer that by saying that only those activities that teach him to be a better person or allow him to serve or help other people are the ones he should pursue—assuming that he also does some things just for fun! I suggest that young people limit their extracurricular activites to two or three besides school and church.

Help him formulate his priorities and his philosophy of life. Most thoughtful parents would like their teen to focus on being well rounded. This might entail being in groups that included the following six types of activities:

Character growth. Activities that encourage this need to be at the top of the list. Reading the Bible, being involved in service groups in church or the community, or joining a charity can be a wonderful means of growing spiritually and developing healthy character.

Emotional awareness. I also think that young people need to be involved in activities that increase their awareness of emotions—their own and others'. Most group activities, in that they require getting along with others and negotiating problems, can help teens understand interpersonal dynamics.

Creativity. Your child needs to develop his sense of imagination and creativity. Any task that can help your child discover unique talents and abilities is important. Many extracurricular activities such as band, orchestra, the arts, yearbook committee, and so on, focus on creative pursuits.

Intellectual development. Though this tends to be focused

in school, students also benefit from enrichment at home or elsewhere. Thus, you might want to encourage a child to be exploring various computer games, searching the Internet for answers to questions (with appropriate adult supervision), or participating in a math or literature quiz group. In addition, many of the things a child does in creative pursuits or service projects require intellectual skills.

Social interests. Your child needs to be in some activities that will help him learn to get along with a variety of people, rather than sticking with one particular crowd. Girl Scouts and Boy Scouts often capitalize on this, trying to form diverse groups of kids and help them get along together.

Physical development. Promoting physical development is the same as promoting good health. If your child has gym daily at school or is generally an active child, you don't need to worry so much about this. But kids who tend towards being "couch potatoes" would benefit from some sort of regular exercise. This can be as unstructured as a family game of badminton or as structured as a community soccer program.

Finally, make sure your child knows that *fun* is a valuable activity that is absolutely essential to life. And having fun means having enough free time to play. Time to play, think, imagine, meditate, and just exist, is what each of us needs and many of us don't get. Help your teen to think through his priorities and choose activities of the right sort and number to promote personal growth.

PARENT-TEEN COMMUNICATION

My fifteen-year-old son is going through what I call the "grunt" stage. It just seems so hard to get him to talk about school or girls or anything. How can I get him to communicate? He'll have periods when

he's very open, but in between, silence. When I ask too many questions, he thinks I'm prying.

That letter reminds me so much of my own daughter. When she was fourteen years of age, she and I were really at odds with one another. I changed my working schedule so that I could be at home when she got home from school. I had the juice and the potato chips (or cookies or whatever I thought might appeal to her) handy, and the stage was set for us to have a wonderful time of communicating. Except, unfortunately, that just did not happen. I would ask her how lunch was that day, and I would get, like this mother, a grunt. I would ask how a test was, and I got another monosyllabic answer, one that I couldn't really interpret one way or the other. Before long, she was off to her room and all chance for communication was lost. I was hurt beyond measure, because I loved her very much, and I felt her slipping away from me.

Fortunately, I asked God's guidance and that of a great many friends and came to an understanding of what was going wrong. As a matter of fact, my daughter herself told me. She said one day, "Mother, you are absolutely yucky! You ought to know that I am not four years old, and you can't talk to me like you did when I was four. I'm fourteen." And to her, fourteen was pretty old. Even though she sounded a bit rude, I understood what she was saying, and I quit trying to talk to her as if she were a child. I looked through my days desperately for any event or subject that I thought would be of interest to her. The next day after school, over a soft drink, I said, "Kathy, let me tell you what happened to me today." And I told her a story that was somewhat funny. It was a miracle, because I hadn't yet finished the story, when she said, "Oh, Mom, did that really happen to you? Let me tell you what happened to me." And we were off to a major change in our relationship.

Judaism has a marvelous ritual. It is called the *bar mitzvah* or *bas mitzvah.* At this time young people celebrate the transition from childhood into the adult world with a religious ceremony. The children know rather clearly when the child stops being a child and becomes a young adult. In non-Jewish families, we can develop this transition, much as I tried to do with my daughter. It is largely a state of mind. My invitation of my daughter into my adult life was my sharing with her the events of my days.

Share feelings, events, and thoughts with your child. I think you will find that he in turn will share with you. Express interest without prying. Understanding your adolescent is so important if you are to grow to become adult friends in the years to follow.

SHOPLIFTING

How serious or common is the problem of teenage shoplifting?

The problem is very common, and unfortunately it is not limited to teenagers. There has been a great rise in shoplifting even among the elderly in our society. Many stores now have store detectives to pick up those shoplifters. If I were a parent who had a shoplifting teenager, I would be grateful if he got caught the very first time around, because getting caught can create a healthy fear and honest respect for the law.

Perhaps more important than what a parent is to do is understanding why kids shoplift.

One of the reasons is that they are craving excitement, and somehow it becomes a bit of a cat-and-mouse game. "Can I get this bit of makeup?" or "Can I take the flashlight without anyone realizing that I have it?"

Testing the limits of authority is another reason for young peoples' stealing. Pitting their cleverness against the mentality of the shopowners is a challenge. Very rarely do these kids need the items that they are stealing.

The most common shoplifters are those from affluent families. They seem to need attention, to be noticed, and that prompts many misbehaviors, including shoplifting. Almost always, in my experience, the habitual shoplifter feels unloved, unimportant, unattended to by parents or other significant adults. This does not mean the parents actually do *not* love them, the kids just do not *feel* that they are loved.

Some thieves are unsuccessful people who somehow feel that they can achieve a sense of importance through shoplifting.

A great many young people also steal to support drug habits, and that's a very strong motivator.

If your child has been caught shoplifting, require that child to return the item at once. If she has used the item or damaged it, so it cannot be returned, require her to earn the money to pay for it. Evaluate your family, including yourselves; see if your teen is getting enough attention and positive affirmation. If not, take steps to begin to correct this. Also check out her friends. See if any might be a bad influence on her. And remember, mistakes are forgivable—by you and by God. Make sure that your child knows that.

DANGER SIGNS

What are some of the signs that would tell parents that their son or daughter had a very serious emotional problem or was becoming suicidal?

There are a great number of young people who have committed suicide in the last decade. In many cases, their lives could have been saved had their parents known these signs and responded appropriately:

Physical Signs. These are the first and easiest to define.

These signs include a major departure from the child's usual physical patterns, such as a change in eating habits. This may mean the child who has normally eaten fairly regular meals begins eating excessively or nothing at all. It can be either extreme and that is important to observe. The same is true of sleeping. A child may sleep excessively or a decreased amount. *Any major change* is worthy of your notice.

Social Signs. They may withdraw into their own room and their own little world. They may escape into excessive activities in order to avoid emotional pain. They may become rude and irritable or extremely polite. Again, it is the variation from that child's own unique norm that is worthy of consideration.

Emotional Indicators. Any marked change from the child's normal status should be noted: a child who becomes irritable when usually he has been fairly mild mannered; depressed when he has usually been happy; excited when he has usually been quiet; unusually worried, anxious, or moody. All of these are signs to be noted.

Personal Habits. These also need looking at. Giving away special treasures, leaving a will or notes that seem to be accidentally left around, or deterioration of work at school— these are all signs that can help parents to know a child is sad, angry, or in danger.

I hope that you will be aware of your child's behaviors in all of these areas of his life. Do not hesitate *if there is any concern* to seek the advice of a competent family counselor. Get the help that you and your child may need—before it is too late! Your troubled child may "clam up" and act like he doesn't want to be bothered. Do not be deceived by this! Without lecturing or nagging, be persistent. Say, "I can read the worry and sadness in your face. Please tell me about your concerns. There's no problem our love and God's wisdom can't solve." Give him a bit of time and space, but stick with him (or her) until the problem is solved!

PARENT BURNOUT

Right now I'm experiencing emotional burnout because I am the father of three teenagers, including twins in junior high. They are all strongly expressing their need for independence. Can you suggest something that will help me bear up under all the pressure?

Being a parent is not only a twenty-four-hour job, it's a lifetime assignment with few, if any, vacations! Here are some practical suggestions that I would like to leave with this dad and others. Perhaps they will be helped to find joy again in being parents.

1. Take time for yourself! Spend time with a friend or alone, take a day or a weekend off occasionally and do exactly what you would like to do. Visit someone out of state, or stay in a nearby hotel or retreat center. But make sure your needs for solitude, fun, sleep, and so on are all adequately met.

2. Find ways to be friends with your teenagers! Share your experiences and feelings with them on a daily basis. Let them see you as a human being—a friend. The major developmental task of teenagers is learning to become independent. Your teens are right on target in "expressing their need for independence." If you try too hard to control them, you will be in constant conflict. Try a new approach instead by becoming friends.

3. Let your teens know your needs. Ask them for comfort and reassurance. Let them give you a back rub or be a sounding board for you regarding some problem about which they may have some helpful suggestions.

4. Spend one-on-one time with each child. There's a lot of good communication that can occur that way.

5. Laugh together. Lots of tension can be relieved with a little bit of humor.

6. Share. Allow your teens to share some of your burdens.

Let them grow into new privileges. Suggest to your children, "Let's all do the basement or garage on Saturday, and then we'll play baseball or go fishing." Or, "If you kids will do the yard really well, we'll all do something special this evening." This often makes work more of a pleasure.

Show interest in them, their friends, their activities, their likes and dislikes, and avoid condemning them, and you will relate to your teens with greater ease. At this time, you will not be able to pound your values into them, but you can at least demonstrate your values through the joy of your own life.

DECISION MAKING

Things seemed to be so much easier before adolescence. Now making decisions with my daughter is fraught with danger.

You're right. Decision making with teens is a whole new ball game, and parents need to change gears. They can no longer just go their way and tell their kids what is going to happen. Here are some suggestions.

Use *thought,* rather than *emotions.* Young people are very emotional, and parents are too, but when those emotions clash, decision making does not come out very well. So be careful that you keep your feelings in control, and keep your decision thoughtful. Determine to make your decision on the basis of what is right for you and for your child. Not *who* is right, but *what* is right, is important.

As much as possible, keep the decision making with your teenager a democratic process, so that you are not seen as a dictator. Teach your teen how to define her options, see their consequences, and decide on a course of action. Be sure to allow her, in most cases, to experience the consequences of her decisions (both bad and good) so she will learn from them. If your teenager simply cannot come to a healthy decision, then you must exercise your parental authority.

LEAVING THE NEST

I'd like to know how to get our kids to move out after they are twenty-one. We love them, but we're worried because they seem quite satisfied to remain with us. Are we helping or hurting them by allowing them to stay?

A great many parents share this concern. Let us think for a minute about why it is that young people want to stay at home. Sometimes they need more warmth, nurturing, and attention— they simply haven't become saturated with their childhood dependency needs. Sometimes there is fear and insecurity— they wonder if they can make it on their own. A great many young people are afraid, especially in today's economy, of financial failure. Sometimes young people stay home out of selfishness and greed. ("I don't want to spend my money on food and housing. It's easier to let Mom and Dad take care of me and foot the bill.") Sometimes it's just downright laziness. ("Mom cooks, cleans, and launders for me. Why should I leave and have to do all of those things for myself?")

Let me make some suggestions that will help you decide whether your children are going to grow up and leave home, or perhaps still stay on.

I suggest that you begin *charging them a realistic amount of rent.* Likewise, charge for the services that you provide. Make this amount a fair one, not just symbolic. Help your children find resources other than Mom and Dad to meet their needs. They may, for example, find some of their emotional needs met by friends, activities, or hobbies. Withdraw your parenting and nurturing just a bit so they won't have quite so much satisfaction from you as parents. Stop serving them quite so adequately. Push them toward independence, even while they are at home, and ask that they help you some.

Then I suggest you *discuss your feelings* honestly with them. Some children believe that their parents want them to stay, and they need to know that you're ready for some independence and freedom, too. Let them know that you would like them to move out and be on their own.

Finally, work with them to *set a fair and realistic deadline* for them to move out, and then help them pack. Help them find a place to go, brag about their moves toward independence, and invite them back now and then. But do insist that they acquire their independence and you your freedom.

5

FAMILY RELATIONSHIPS

PRESSURED DAD

My wife and I want to do the best job possible of raising our daughters, and we try to spend a lot of time together as a family. But one thing that really bothers us is that while people expect my wife to make changes in her life for the girls, a man isn't supposed to. My friends at work don't seem to understand why I don't hang around the office any longer than necessary. A couple of guys even have said that I am hurting my future. But I feel like I'm doing a good job and not cutting corners on my work. Do you have any suggestions?

Studies in recent years show that fathers are key figures in the lives of both girls and boys. So this father is right to fight for time for his family.

My first suggestion is that you try to get a sense from your supervisor or boss about whether taking on extra projects is expected for promotion or for maintaining your current job. Without talking specifically about family concerns, try to come to a clear understanding with your boss so your mind can be at rest. Most bosses will respect a desire to identify job expectations but many will not be able to accept a father's saying that his family concerns have the potential of affecting his work.

Be quite certain in your own mind of your priorities. Then you can take the jibes of your friends without letting them bother you. I have recently heard of several men and women who have turned down major advancements in jobs in the interests of their children, and I respect that immensely. Such determination and courage portray to me real strength of character, wisdom, and great love. It is not as necessary to advance in your job when your children are small as it is to advance the interests of your children themselves. I cannot emphasize enough what a major influence fathers are in the lives of their children.

TOO STRICT DAD

The problem my husband and I are now facing is that I think he is too strict with our children, especially our two year old. His own dad was extremely strict to the point that my husband often wished him dead. Do you have anything to say that might help us both come to a good and reasonable way of raising our children?

The way parents are raised is so often the way they raise their children. In this family, I am concerned about the unbalanced parenting. The father seems strict and extreme, whereas the mother is more lenient and soft. In such parenting, a vicious cycle can get going. The harsher and more strict one parent is, the more lenient and sympathetic the other becomes. There are two results that can evolve: first, parents get at odds with one another; and second, the child gets caught in the middle.

Parents, above all, do not get in angry fights about your child or his discipline in front of him. That can create a great deal of fear and guilt in the child. In this specific case, I would recommend that the mother try to help the husband recall how he felt as a child. But don't do that while he is upset with either you or the child. When he is relaxed and calm and perhaps feeling a little remorseful, help him remember his own feelings and help him identify with your child. Gently, but clearly, guide your husband to see that his son could be developing feelings like the ones he had for his dad. Aid your family in building love, respect, and enjoyment of each other. When your child is able and Dad is calm, have him honestly tell Dad how he feels when Dad is too harsh or strict.

Do protect your children from abuse, but as much as possible, stay out of the middle. Having the children go directly to the father without Mother can help Dad to really hear the pain that he is inflicting on that child. Comment to your husband on insights that you have gleaned from articles and books. Unfortunately, I find that many men do not read parenting books, but if your husband *will* read such material, give him books and articles on childrearing that can help him understand child development. A book might aid your husband in better understanding the turbulent two-year-old stage.

Above all else, do not set yourself up as the authority, the right one. That can create such a feeling of inferiority and inadequacy that he may give up and not even try to be involved in the parenting. When he does well, finds patience, and treats the child wisely, praise him and let him know how much you appreciate his efforts. Mothers and fathers must pull together.

FATHER'S APPROVAL

I am anxious to ask you about children and low self-

esteem. My seven-year-old daughter has a problem in this area. She has a lot of God-given talents which we praise. She's a good girl, and I tell her that I'm glad God gave her to me as my child. But I'm wondering if her confidence would be greater if her father praised her more.

This mother has a very important concern, and I can hardly emphasize enough how vital it is to build this healthy self-confidence in children. Let me explain clearly and concisely what parents need to do.

Both parents must work together. The child needs praise from her father as well as her mother. If both parents understand how vital self-esteem is, they can pull together in a successful fashion.

1. First, build success for the child by assigning tasks and projects that she is realistically capable of doing, or pay special attention to things she is already doing.

2. Help her with those tasks by sticking with her lovingly, but also by firmly and sternly (if need be) encouraging her until she does those jobs the very best she can.

3. Praise what the child does honestly and point out simply and *specifically* what was good about the job. Avoid just saying, "You did a good job." Be more clear and detailed: "I like the color you put in the sky, and the way the tree looks like it's waving." Give a lot of verbal approval. Tell your child what it is you particularly like about the way she acts, how she looks, and what she does. Remember, it's easy to overlook the routine, wonderful things your child does well every day unless you make a point of commenting.

Be careful that one parent does not try to balance out the other's sternness by sympathizing or overprotecting a child. The affirmation of both parents will complete the child's needs for approval. Build together the self-esteem that will make your child's life a success, and that means both parents working as a team!

COMPARISONS

Our twelve-year-old boy has a problem with low self-esteem. I think it's due to his older brother and sister, who both do well in school. When this son was younger, he showed much affection and an outgoing nature. But he's developed an attitude that he can't measure up.

This mother has a beautifully perceptive attitude. I would recommend that she use her perceptiveness to benefit her child who is struggling with poor self-esteem due to the accomplishments of his siblings. This often happens when one child excels in academic areas and another does not. But the fact is that each child can excel somewhere. We just have to find that place.

I remember one teenager who was ordered by juvenile court to see me. He had been getting into all sorts of trouble, and he seemed very unmoved by it. He did not seem to want to change, and I could find nothing that he was interested in that might motivate him (except things he could not have). But he found the answer! One week he came in, not dragging his feet as usual, but with a big smile on his face. He brought a bike racing trophy he had just won. He hid it inside his jacket and brought it out slowly, with great drama, to show me. He had fixed up an old BMX-style bike that he'd found. The father of a friend of his offered to take him along to races with his own son. The boy entered and started winning. I knew then that this boy would succeed. He had found something in life he wanted.

Every child has a spark within him of something he can do well. That's what you need to find for your son. Apparently his spark is not in academic areas, at least not so far. Then look elsewhere. Does he like to work with his hands? Does he like sports? or collecting things? Maybe he'd enjoy a hobby like model trains or building wooden ships or collecting rocks. Maybe he can run fast and would benefit from a local track program. Or perhaps he likes to fish or bowl or do gymnastics. Maybe he's a natural salesman and would enjoy earning money through sales programs open to young people, or perhaps he's an actor or singer or gardener. Look around for what sorts of activities are available to him and affordable for you.

Get him out of the shadows of his siblings' limelight and into his own spotlight. Encourage his siblings to affirm him, as well, and you have a recipe for success.

ONLY CHILD

What effect does being an only child have on personal growth and development? And how can parents compensate for a child's having no brothers or sisters?

An only child can become rather selfish. She can expect (more than the child with brothers and sisters) that the whole world revolves around her and her needs. Yet there are many ways parents can compensate for that.

Some of the advantages of having siblings can be worked out through friends. Certainly one of the wonderful things I enjoyed with my brothers and sisters was the fact that we had built-in *playmates* and friends. Working, arguing, and playing together were fine experiences of my childhood. Learning to share, to take turns, to be considerate, are qualities of life that brothers and sisters can teach one another. For the only child, friends can be imported to play those roles. The friends should not be sent home as soon as the children argue. Instead, encourage them to work things out and learn more about getting along.

Another benefit is healthy *competition.* My family regularly played games together. However, again friends can fulfill some of that role with an only child. Parents can also play games with a child, teaching the only child about winning, losing, and taking turns.

There is also a *security* related to having a larger family that's supportive and fun. My brothers, sisters, and I still enjoy a great deal of mutual support when we get together. You might perhaps seek cousins or other nearby relatives to fulfill this particular role in the life of an only child. Some children spend a lot of time with cousins by visiting together during the summer or school vacations. Some families share summer homes or recreational vehicles that bring them together. Some grandparents also open their homes so the grandchildren can visit all at once. Thus, at least temporarily, the only child gets to live as though she were part of a large family.

There are also some disadvantages to having brothers and sisters, and these become the advantages of an only child. Sometimes brothers or sisters create a situation of partiality or unfair rivalry and competition in which one is too often the winner and the other a loser. Sometimes the division of the parents' time and attention becomes unfair or unequal, and an only child never has to worry about that particular problem. In a large family children may have to share too much and may lose some of their own identity.

TIME WITH GRANDMOTHER

How much time is too much for a child to spend visiting with a good grandmother? She would love to have her grandchild with her every day if she could.

A good grandparent-child relationship can offer you and your child many things: loving support, sharing of wisdom and experience, fun things to do that parents don't always have time for, and time away from parents without the cost of a sitter.

How much time a child spends with grandparents depends entirely upon the needs of all those involved. Here are some questions to ask when considering how much time:

- Does the child want to spend time with Grandma or Grandpa?
- Do the parents and child have enough time to themselves to establish intimacy and develop family traditions?
- Do the grandparents have enough time to themselves and time to get needed rest and recreation?
- Are the grandparents a positive influence on the child, showing unconditional love and acceptance?
- Do the grandparents affirm your values as parents and confirm those values to your child?
- Does the child ever misbehave after visits to the grandparents, suggesting there are problems? If so, do you know why?
- Are there power struggles between you and the grandparents over your child?
- Do the grandparents indulge the child making a monster out of her when you get her back?

ROLE OF GRANDPARENTS

Several years ago my husband was transferred to Alaska, and that meant being separated from our families by thousands of miles. We felt sad that our children were so far from their grandparents, but we struck up a friendship with some older neighbors, and our children began calling them Grandma and Grandpa. When the children's real

grandparents learned about it, they were very hurt. Can you give me some advice?

I would like to talk a little bit about grandparents in general. I really believe that grandparents' roles in a child's life are priceless. Perhaps that's even an understatement. These specific grandparents are no doubt grieving because they can't be near the family, and they understandably resent other people taking their places and enjoying their roles in the children's lives. The best function of grandparents, in my opinion, is this: the simple acceptance and enjoyment of children without the need to train and discipline and do all of the corrective things that parents must do. Grandparents usually have time to be more patient and understanding than parents do, and that's also very special in a child's life.

Let me say that these grandparents should feel proud that they have played such an important part in their grandchildrens' lives that the family really needs a substitute for them. They may be grateful that others are willing to take over some of the functions they cannot perform. Perhaps there is a family near them which needs a local "grandparent" because the real ones are very far away.

The parents of these children should be careful to teach the children that their biological grandparents are very special. Perhaps they can best do that by using a different name for the foster grandparents. They might perhaps just call them Mr. or Mrs., or Grandpa John and Grandma Mary—any name other than the one that they would use for their own grandparents.

The parents should also make a point to have their children keep in touch with distant grandparents. Have them send them the letters and little pictures that they would give them if they lived nearby. And don't forget the phone, fax machine, and e-mail. Once children begin to write, they can write grandparents on the computer and send the message by e-mail. Pictures can be faxed, and phone calls can be made quick but warm. Grandparents can love and understand the children, and "borrowed" grandparents need not threaten the real ones.

GIFT-BEARING GRANDPARENTS

Many times when my children's grandparents have come to visit, they've brought small gifts, and now my children have gotten into the habit of always expecting gifts. I'm embarrassed when they ask the grandparents what they've brought for them. How can I handle this and keep everybody happy?

A universal rule should be established. The rule is very simple: Children, you do *not* ask your grandparents or any visiting guests for gifts. That isn't hard to understand, and if it's repeated each time those grandparents are going to visit, then the children should be quite clear that this is simply not permitted. Of course, children do forget rules and they may go ahead and ask. If that happens, explain kindly but firmly to both children and grandparents that when they ask, they are not to receive gifts. Gifts are the right of the giver to decide whether or not to give.

Make your own arrangements with the grandparents, too. Ask them to bring gifts only rarely and not to feel compelled to bring things simply because the children have requested them. I think it's very important that children realize that the time and the loving presence of their grandparents are the best gifts of all. And if they get too many material things, they will fail to realize the value of this special kind of love.

Help your children to turn that gift-giving idea around. Help *them* to make a special gift for their grandparents. Children can create very clever craft items. A photograph or some special little item that the child has found on a nature hike can be a wonderful gift to give to grandparents. Giving is indeed a two-way street.

FAMILY LOOK-ALIKES

What kinds of problems can grow out of a child's resemblance to someone else in the family?

It's strange, but nevertheless true, that there are many such problems. I am currently working with a family in which that is the case. The mother has found that from the moment her little girl was born the baby reminded her of her own mother. Unfortunately, she and her mother did not get along very well, and unconsciously she laid on this tiny baby many of the negative qualities that she had experienced from her mother. As the baby grew, Mom had a difficult time liking her.

Parents need to be careful that in looking at their newborn baby and seeing Grandfather's ears or Mother's nose they remember that even though the child has some physical characteristics like those relatives, the child is a separate individual. Be careful to love and accept each child individually for who he is, for what she is like, and separate this child consciously and consistently from other people.

If well-meaning friends comment about family resemblances, have a response ready, such as: "Yes, Jane does look like Aunt Helen. And we like family resemblances. But she is her own person, and we love her for her uniqueness." This will reinforce your unconditional love and help others to see your child for herself.

EFFECT OF DIVORCE

My youngest son, age twelve, was only eight when his dad and I divorced. Sometimes I wonder what the

long-term effect will be. Do you have any suggestions?

Either directly or indirectly, divorce affects a majority of American homes. There are many feelings involved in every divorce—grief over the loss, anger over the rejection, all kinds of very intense, negative, and destructive emotions.

Children are especially vulnerable to those feelings. They rarely get those feelings worked out, because they don't know how to talk about them. They don't have the vocabulary to express them, and their parents are so involved in their own distress that they are often not aware how urgently the children need to deal with those problems.

Fortunately, there are now programs run by schools, churches, and community groups that seek to aid children of divorce. *Rainbows* is one such program. It aims to help children talk about the divorce, recognize that their family is not alone, and build new hopes for the future of their two families. These groups can be especially important for children during the early months of the divorce or separation when emotions in the family are running high and the parents may have difficulty talking calmly about the events in the family.

Recent studies emphasize the importance of fathers as well as mothers. Long-term studies of divorce indicate that the outcome depends largely on how well the custodial parent (if parenting is not shared) handles the divorce and whether the noncustodial parent remains connected and in tune with the child. If your child's father is not involved with your son, then a substitute "dad" or "big brother" would be a good influence. Look among your male relatives, neighbors, and church members to see if you can find someone trustworthy and emotionally healthy who might act as a good buddy for your son. The Big Brother program in many communities links willing adults with boys from single-parent homes.

Once some of the divorce turmoil settles, parents can discuss the topic of divorce with less emotion. Help your child to talk about things that upset him about the divorce. Are there living or visitation arrangements that cause him grief? Are there questions he has about the past, about the circumstances of the divorce? He might not remember much about that time in his life. You might be surprised how little he remembers. Encourage him to talk about his feelings and concerns. He is old enough now to be able to begin to put his feelings into words.

Here are a few more important ideas for helping any child of divorce:

1. Make sure he understands enough about the divorce so that he does not blame himself. (But give no sordid details, please!)

2. Give him permission to love the other parent.

3. Teach him to forgive others when wrongs are done (and work on forgiving your ex-spouse yourself).

4. Be sure not to allow him to manipulate you by using the other parent.

5. Help him to identify the good in both parents and avoid seeing only the bad.

MOVING

I would like to know how we can prepare our nine-year-old daughter for moving to a new town. I know that moving can be upsetting to children, but we have no choice in the matter. She's already concerned about a new school and leaving her friends behind.

Some time ago I came across a shocking statistic that said that the average American moves fourteen times in a lifetime, and that concerns me because I know how disruptive those moves can be.

Such moves are unsettling to children and parents alike. Moving brings about a grief process. Children lose a great many things in such a move. So I recommend that parents try to understand, practice, and teach children about the process of grief.

Include your children in the process. The excitement of a new and different area can be as much a part of any move as grief is. Keep (or make) your own attitude optimistic. Share your plans with your children. Let them have a part in house hunting and selecting a neighborhood. Choose your neighborhood very carefully. It's essential that you find a place where there are good schools, adequate libraries, safe shopping centers, and a fine church so that your children may have the spiritual nurture that they need. In planning for your new home, give the children some votes in redecorating an older home or planning a new one. Certainly in their own rooms or in a common room like a family room, children should have some say in the color scheme or the curtains or bedspreads that are chosen. That will help them to feel a bit more comfortable in the new setting. And don't replace all the furniture, but move the comfortable old things into the new house for gradual replacement if necessary.

Keep all your children's favorite toys and games. Recently I met with a little girl who had had to move from one city to another, and she went through a very grievous time over that move. Tragically, one of the saddest events of all was the loss of her old teddy bear. It was decrepit and ugly, but it was hers, and losing that teddy bear produced a great deal of sadness and anger in her heart.

Make a clean break. I recommend a ceremonious leave-taking when you must move. Have your children exchange some small gifts with friends—a photograph or an old book. A special book donated to the school library, farewell parties, a ceremonious time to say good-bye (even with the tears those times will generate) can make leave-taking easier in the long run. Letters back, occasional phone calls, and visits—all of these can help your children to finish the grief after moving and to be free to allow themselves to enjoy the new home.

MIDDLE CHILD

We have two boys, ages nine and six, and a daughter who is two. My question concerns our second son. He awakens almost every morning irritable and complaining. It seems he can rarely find anything good about any situation. We have tried ignoring his complaining and also being strict about his arguing with us. But his sour outlook and continual testing often leave me frustrated and exhausted, which precipitates a hasty remark that I might leave home because I can't stand him anymore. I guess I need help, too!

Middle children do routinely have a difficult time of it. They have to submit to an often bossy older sibling, give in to a sometimes babied youngest child, and never get to have the total attention of their parents. Furthermore, this boy sounds like his personality traits are all on the extreme end of the scale.

This child sounds like one who may need professional help. And perhaps as much or more than the child, the parents may need professional guidance. When a child reaches a state in which it sounds as if every transaction between the child and the family is a negative, unhappy one, then he has reached a state that parents alone simply cannot correct. But let me give some suggestions to this family so that they might *begin* to turn things around:

First, this mother should list all the resentments and anxieties that she has about her son.

Second, she should think through the areas of resentment and concern, pray about them, and search for some understanding and forgiveness of those traits that are most annoying.

Third, she should list all of the good qualities that she may have overlooked. As she comes across those good qualities in her son's life, she can comment simply but sincerely to him, so that he can begin to see some hope for himself as a good person. Together parents and children can work hard to create a contract for change.

This mother could go by her son's bed at night and tuck him in gently and lovingly. In the morning, she could go and awaken him personally, rather than calling to him, so that he might awaken in a better mood. If she quietly and specifically responds to positive things as she comes across them, she will build up good feelings in her son. Then the two of them can decide together what misbehaviors must go and how they will work out some better behaviors to create loving and positive feelings within the family. As they develop some happy activities together, and build on positive feelings, even the very negative habits that have developed with such a child can be turned into a loving situation within the family.

MAKING A WILL

We're in the process of drawing up a will, and we want to include a statement about who should take care of our minor children if something happens to us. We're wondering if it should be someone in the family or friends who share our interests and have similar lifestyles. Also, would it be better to choose people who already have children?

This is a wise couple. Though making a will is a painful process because no one would like to anticipate his own death, it is a necessity. There are several goals that parents need to consider in developing such a plan for their children.

1. You want your children to have the security and familiarity of their own environment. Unless the children are very young, they should not have to face losing their familiar surroundings as well as their parents. Ideally one would select guardians for them who are close enough that they could continue attending their familiar schools and church. For some families that plan would necessitate the selection of relatives. For others, the neighborhood, the school, the church, and so on could best be maintained by selecting friends who live nearby. For very young children, the consistency of caretaking is much more important than maintaining the same environment. But if you name a guardian three states away when your first child is born, you should be prepared to change your will as your children grow and enter school.

2. A second consideration is the values that you deem most important for your children. Whom do you know that will teach these same values to your children? Again, for some of you this may be relatives. For others who do not share the same values as your relatives, you may find friends could best maintain that goal for your children.

3. Further, you should consider the ability of the couple to manage children. Though Grandma and Grandpa may have been excellent parents for you, will they still have the youth and energy required to raise another set of children if you name them as guardians? Or should you select someone younger but childless? I believe that couples who have their own children can usually understand and adapt to other children more easily than people who have had no children at all. So, this is something to consider.

Whomever you choose, I would recommend that you do this by formulating a plan. Cultivate those people as friends. Spend time together so that they and your children will get to know, love, understand, and trust each other. If there are major differences or a lack of respect, it may help you decide to choose a different family. Offer a simple explanation of your plan to your children, so they understand who this special family may be in their lives, but avoid worrying your children or making them fearful of losing you.

PREPARING CHILD FOR NEW PARENT

What guidelines do you recommend for getting a stepparent/stepchild relationship off to a good start? My three-year-old daughter will soon have a stepmom in the house.

Many parents and children are facing new relationships due to divorce or bereavement. The issues that are at stake are these:

- her father's time and energy focused on the new spouse
- the sense of displacement or rejection the daughter may feel
- the sense of rejection the new spouse may feel if the child does not take naturally to her
- the sense of disloyalty to her biological mother (how can she love a new mommy, when she still loves her old mommy?)
- changes in lifestyle and family routines that will come from the new mother

Handling these issues is not so simple. Try keeping these principles in mind as you attempt to build a positive relationship between stepchild and stepparent.

Give information. Explain and explain and explain again! Do not take for granted that the child will understand the new living arrangement and the advent of a new mommy. Help her to know that she doesn't have to choose between her "old" mother and the new one. She can love both of them and treat them each in her own way. Sometimes this process is helped along by choosing a name for the new mother that does not compete with the "old" mother. If a child can distinguish the two by name, then she will feel less disloyal to her biological parent.

Keep an open mind. The stepparent should not expect any specific behavior. Explore who this child is and what your relationship can be. Think about what you have to offer this girl and what the child has to give to you.

Identify the good points. What are the good points about that child's biological parent? It's very easy for a stepparent to subtly compete with a child's absent mother or father, and to find out bad things about him or her in order to appear better. Avoid that at all costs.

Understand that child's losses. Your new stepchild is probably feeling grief, confusion, and anger over the loss of a parent in death or divorce. The child will often tend to cover sad, tender feelings with aggression and acting out in a rude and unkind way. By understanding the child's tender feelings, anxieties, and concerns, you will not feel personally affronted or hurt by the child's misbehaviors or her reluctance to accept you. Instead, you can help her through those difficult feelings by labeling them and interpreting them.

Focus on unconditional acceptance. Concentrate on kind, honest, and complete acceptance of the child. That doesn't mean you must put up with rude or disrespectful behavior, but that you understand the child's honesty with you and accept that. Encourage the child to talk out the feelings that she has for you, as well as for her natural parent. Treat the child as you would a dear, young friend.

Earn respect. Do not expect an immediate parent/child relationship. Work toward earning that while you are developing a friendship. Allow the child to approach you, and be available. But don't demand a sudden intimacy or response, because that simply cannot happen. Move slowly into parenting. Any changes in rules should be explained in detail to the child by the biological parent.

Expect divided loyalty. Such manipulation can come about when the child tries to play her parent against the new person in the house. If you expect this, you will be ready to handle it by refusing to compete with the other parent, by not tolerating the child's manipulations, by staying together as adults, and by working together for the child's sake. Tough as it is to create a new family together, both you and your child can do it.

FALSE GUILT

I am now working outside of our home after being able to be home with our children for six years. We have a wonderful sitter, but some days the guilt of not being home is too much.

Let me define the difference between *real guilt* and *false guilt.* Real guilt comes when we know we have done something wrong. If you have been too harsh on your children or if you have made mistakes in judgment and punished them for something that they never did, then certainly you will feel guilty. That's fairly easy to correct by admitting the mistake, apologizing, and making it right. False guilt comes when we feel that we have done something wrong, but we honestly cannot define what it is. That false guilt is what it seems this mother is suffering.

Most mothers who work outside the home feel a number of conflicts about that. In most cases they have been raised to believe that mothers should be at home full-time until their children are teenagers or college students. Yet, because that value was often not openly stated while they were growing up, many women struggle to understand why they feel guilty about working outside the home. They feel confused.

I suggest that you explain how you feel to both your children and your husband. Let the children know that you're working because you must, and let your husband know that you are glad you can give financial support and help with household needs.

Then, work on building your family into a cooperative unit. Hold a family conference, explain the needs that each of you has, and let each one feel a vital part of meeting those needs. List all of the household and yard tasks, and assign them appropriately and fairly to members of the family. This will give your children and your husband a priceless sense of their value, and your appreciation for their input will help to build a great foundation for their self-esteem and your relationship together.

On a regular basis, share the interesting parts of your job with the family. Try not to complain too much, but share the funny or even the not-so-funny parts of your job.

Work out a schedule that will allow time for all of you to play together as a family. Working outside of the home need not be bad for you or your children. In fact, some families have worked their schedules in a way that both Mom and Dad have one-on-one time with the children. For example, Dad could work during the day and Mom stay home, so she is with the children after school. Then Mom works in the evening or on weekends, and Dad is home so the kids will look to him for their needs. This can help them build the same kind of close relationship with Dad that they probably have with Mom. I feel Dads are *so* important for kids.

6

HEALTH AND NUTRITION

HEADACHES

What is the most common cause of a child's headache?

Headaches in children are usually caused by physical conditions. Emotional stress runs a close second as a cause.

Any child who has a cold, fever, or another *illness* is likely to have a headache. A stuffed-up nose causes you to have a headache, and your child is no different from you. Allergies often cause headaches, too. Along with nasal congestion and watery eyes, there frequently is a headache that accompanies chronic allergies.

Cutting new *teeth* or having infected teeth can cause headaches. Even little babies can experience irritability from this.

In school-age children *eyestrain* may be a problem and cause headaches.

There are *emotional* and psychological problems, too, that can cause headaches. Anxiety, worry, or fear due to family burdens can bring about headaches. (Sometimes you as parents do not even realize that your child is worried about family concerns.)

Sometimes your child's headaches may be due to a certain sense of *anxiety or tension.* Some children are so conscientious and responsible that they try too hard to make good grades, or to get along well, or to do the right thing. Muscular tension in the neck and the forehead stretches and tightens the scalp, which actually is a large tendon. This kind of muscular stretching can cause a very definite pain, which may be due to emotional tension.

Muscle tension can also result from incorrect *posture.* We all know that children sit in some very odd positions while watching TV or playing on the computer. If your child is getting headaches, make sure that this is not an issue.

I have seen children now and then who have had headaches out of *pretense.* The headaches get them out of particular jobs that they do not like or get them attention they want.

What can you do to help your child who has a headache? First, of course, have the child medically checked. Take the child to the doctor to be certain that there is no serious physical problem that is causing the pain. Then provide plenty of loving attention and happy times, along with stress reduction, while requiring the child to be responsible in spite of those headaches.

STOMACHACHE

What are the most common causes of a child's stomachache?

Though many of us may remember using stomachaches to get out of doing dishes, homework, or whatever the job might be, in my family those excuses rarely worked, and they shouldn't work in your home either. There are some physical causes, however, that parents must not overlook.

One of the most common causes of pain is that of either *hunger* or *overeating.* Severe hunger pains are something relatively few people in our country know well, but we do experience pangs when it's getting close to mealtime. Overeating and stretching the stomach can cause serious pain, and can be a problem that may even cause vomiting in some children. Be careful how much food you allow your child to eat at one sitting.

The second cause of stomachaches is *food intolerance* or allergies. Perhaps all of us have eaten certain foods that have caused stomach pain or discomfort. Those foods need to be avoided, and that kind of stomachache can be easily cured. Having trouble with the bowels can also cause stomachaches. Constipation or an excess amount of intestinal gas causes discomfort for many children. Give your children enough water and plenty of fruit in their diets, and constipation should not become a serious problem.

Stomach *flu* is another common cause of stomachaches. Usually that kind of stomach pain is accompanied by persistent vomiting or severe diarrhea and cramping. All of that usually passes within twelve to twenty-four hours, but if it is prolonged, you may need medical care to be sure that your child does not become dehydrated.

The aftermath of a course of *antibiotics* for strep throat or some other infection can also result in a stomachache. This sort of stomachache is often associated with diarrhea or excessive intestinal gas. It can be treated very simply by giving your child yogurt or cultured buttermilk (if you can get the child to drink it) to reintroduce to the digestive tract the normal, healthy bacteria that are contained in those dairy products.

Many *other illnesses* are associated with stomachaches. Strep throat, measles (which we rarely see anymore), and other illnesses may, as part of their onset, be accompanied by a stomachache. It's rare that we see intestinal parasites and pinworms, but those can cause stomach discomfort as well.

The really serious stomachache, which you need to be aware

of, is that of *appendicitis*. With that there is a fever of 100 degrees or more and generalized pain that settles in the right lower fourth of the abdomen and causes severe pain when you press on the abdominal muscles or when such pressure is released (called "rebound pain").

Last of all, children can have stomachaches due to *stress* or attempts to manipulate parents that result in ongoing conflicts. When children live with excessive punishment or *abuse,* they are likely to suffer frequent stomachaches.

Whether your child's stomachache is real or imagined, physical or functional, giving tender, loving care will often aid the proper cure.

CAUSES OF COLDS

The current theory that exposure to dampness, wind, or chills has nothing to do with a youngster getting a cold has me wondering why colds often occur after exposure. What is your opinion?

Saying that colds have nothing to do with dampness or chill is a little misleading. It's true that if a person goes out in the cold and damp and has no contact with cold-causing germs or viruses, then the temperature alone will not cause infection. However, colds are caused by viruses that are harbored within our nostrils or throats, and when we are chilled or fatigued our resistance is lowered, and those viruses can cause an infection. *Cold viruses* multiply and grow in colder temperatures. So, getting chilled or being in a cold climate does have something to do with catching colds. In addition to encouraging the growth of viruses, being chilled alters the circulatory patterns of the body. Getting chilled makes the blood vessels on the surface of the skin constrict. The superficial tissues, therefore, are less well supplied with circulation, and the blood cells that fight off infection are not at the spot where they are most needed.

Colds (or any upper respiratory infection) are caused by three basic infectious agents: viruses (the most common type), bacteria, or a combination of viruses and bacteria. *Viruses* are so numerous that we haven't even discovered all of them. They are a little harder to identify than bacteria, and they cause a less serious infection as a rule, but those infections cannot be treated by antibiotics as bacterial infections can be. Our own bodies have to fight off viral infections. Many people jokingly say that viral colds last a week if they're treated vigorously or seven days if they are not treated at all. So, just give your child plenty of rest, warmth, and lots of juices.

Bacteria are easily identified under the microscope and cause infection with fever, headaches, vomiting, and generally more severe symptoms. The nasal discharge or sputum from a bacterial infection is a yellow or green color, rather than the clear or white discharge of a viral infection. These infections should usually be treated with antibiotics. If in doubt about what your child has, consult your physician.

NO MEDICINE, PLEASE

Some weeks back, my daughter told me she read that some doctors advise a mild sedative for infants who fight sleep. She was really surprised. It would seem one could always be giving a baby some sedative—first for fussiness, then for teething, then for the first day of school!

I certainly appreciate this query, and I respect the intent with which it was asked. In these days when medical science has made so many dramatic advances, it's easy to think that the answer to any ache or discomfort is to take a pill.

All of life is a matter of finding the right balance if we are to live successfully. In medicine, that balance can be very delicate indeed. When I hear from parents who are exhausted and fatigued because their child keeps them up night after night, then I know that those parents and children might be developing a vicious cycle of resentment that may cause serious problems later on. For such parents, I would prescribe medicine that will help break that vicious cycle. However, I also agree with avoiding pills for any whim that comes along. Knowing what and when to prescribe for a troubled child, a sick child, or a family, is a medical issue that demands the good judgment of parent and physician together. For the majority of healthy babies and resourceful parents, no medication is needed. God made our bodies with a tendency toward recovery and health.

PROBLEM-SOLVING RESOURCES

Many parents feel all alone when health problems arise. But they're not, are they?

A school consulted me recently regarding a young student there. He was having epileptic seizures. He was horribly embarrassed by that, and the school officials did not know how to handle it. When I talked with the boy and his father, I discovered that they had had no medical care for at least six years. They didn't have very much money and were unfamiliar with community resources. With only two telephone calls, we were able to put the boy and his father in touch with a clinic where the child had a complete neurological workup. He was put on medication that cost them nothing until the father found a job. The child came back to school, and the seizures were under control. The resources were there; the family simply did not know how to find them.

There are good resources in most communities in the United States. If you are looking for help, first try your family's physician. Your pastor will also know about community programs, and almost all schools have a school counselor or nurse who can refer you for help in specialized areas.

There are area health and mental-health centers that are low cost and extremely supportive for physical, emotional, and psychological problems. In addition, there are specific foundations, such as those for alcoholism, cancer, birth defects, and other problems. These are available to provide help simply for the asking. Most are listed in your phone book.

Don't forget relatives and friends who care and are willing to help in many ways. I find the problem with a great many families is that they are afraid to ask for help. They believe they should be able to go it alone, and then they become hopeless and feel there is nothing anyone can do anyway. But don't despair. Help *is* available. Just ask.

SERIOUS EATING PROBLEM

What do I do about a child who just won't eat anything nutritious?

Usually the eating problems parents encounter with their children are relatively unimportant, and many of them pass with time. Sometimes, however, an unwillingness to eat certain types of food can threaten a child's health.

Eating problems, if they are to occur, almost always begin in early childhood. More often than not, they have less to do with food than they do with power struggles—a battleground that gets established between children and parents. And this is one battle parents really will not win. I will never forget the time that I fed my youngest child the last few bites of egg, and later on (in fact, an hour later), when I took her to my office for her measles immunization shot, and she opened her mouth to cry, I found those same eggs still in her mouth! I had "made" her eat them, but she had proved to me that she would not swallow them! Let me offer some suggestions here that will help you avoid power struggles over food.

Most little children have a built-in sense of what they need to eat in order to stay healthy. Left to their own devices, children will eat a balanced diet over a period of several days. Perhaps at first they may eat a great many fats—that must be what their little systems need. Later on, they'll eat more protein, and still later more vegetables. On a daily basis their diets may look lopsided, but the end result is balanced. Therefore, parents can give their children a bit of freedom with regard to what they eat. Of course, offer them all of the types of food that they need, but then give them freedom to choose, and do not set up a power struggle over eating. If you are concerned about nutrition, give her a daily vitamin.

I advise parents to start with foods that their child really likes and that all of you enjoy. Make the mealtime as pleasant as possible. Set an example of eating a little bit of all of the foods that are prepared. Discourage overly sweet snacks and snacks just before a meal, but make sure that there are healthy and easy-to-eat foods available between meals if your child gets hungry. Offer small servings at mealtime and add more as the child's appetite increases. If a child vigorously objects to something served, consider allowing that child to substitute something from the same food group that is more acceptable to him or her (so long as the parent does not have to cook anything extra). For example, raw carrots could be substituted for the squash the child does not like, or tuna fish could replace liver. Do not nag or punish the child. Be kind and loving, and mealtimes will be seen as pleasant experiences.

In contrast to the minor issues that arise with very young children, eating problems in older children can be much more serious. A child who may have been in a power struggle with Mom or Dad early in childhood, in later childhood or adolescence can develop an eating disorder. We are seeing a great many young people today who suffer from *anorexia nervosa* and *bulimia.* These are preteens and teens, mostly girls, who limit food intake and exercise excessively, or who binge eat and get rid of the food by inducing vomiting or using laxatives. These young people always, in my experience, have some very deep-seated emotional problems that require professional counseling and outside help. If you find your child abusing laxatives, locking herself in the bathroom and vomiting, or becoming obsessed with dieting and exercise, seek help from your pediatrician immediately.

OVERWEIGHT CHILD

My five-year-old daughter is overweight. Should I put her on a diet, or should I just cut out all the goodies? I don't want her to feel deprived, but she will start school in September and I'm worried about her being teased.

If this child is indeed seriously overweight, then her mother has a valid concern. But before taking any action, I would want her mother to discuss with her pediatrician whether the child is overweight. Weights can vary widely, and children at this age often seem chubby. But a child who does not have a serious problem will not be helped by a mother who is fussing over weight.

If the child is truly overweight, then this mother's concern is valid. We know that a major problem for adults begins with the existence of excessive fat cells, even from infancy, in children who tend to be overweight. These fat cells are larger and more numerous than in other people, so the tendency to be fat is a lifelong problem once it becomes established. This parent should look for reasons why this child is overeating. Understanding those reasons can help this mother correct the problem.

One of the reasons children overeat is due to *loneliness* or *boredom*. I find that children who are afraid of others, who don't have enough playmates or other activities, who spend a lot of time alone or watching TV, tend to eat almost as a recreational activity. Often there is a family pattern of overeating. In our culture, eating has come to have many symbolic meanings. It can represent security, intimacy, comfort, celebration—all kinds of emotional needs can seem to be met through eating.

Overeating also may be due to a *contest of wills*. The child may see this as a means of getting even with a parent who is too controlling (as the child sees it).

The solution to overeating, therefore, becomes dependent on understanding the reasons. Once you discover why your child overeats, you can correct the underlying problem. For example, find active playmates so your child can be more active, or enroll her in sports such as gymnastics, swimming, or soccer (all of which may be available at low cost through community programs). Help her to join in the fun with her friends so she will not think about eating. And give her plenty of warm, loving attention. Keep her mind off foods by your own presence in her life.

Creative activities can also help. Getting her hands busy helps her mouth to be much less actively engaged. Help her to color, paint, or model with clay. Take her on long walks or nature hikes to change her focus.

Plan the menu for your family to be lower in fat. Provide more raw vegetables and fruits along with your usual fare. Cut down on sugars and desserts. Offer her a small vegetable and cheese snack between meals and at bedtime, so that the child will not become overly hungry before mealtimes. Limit second helpings to low-calorie foods. Serve your child's plate, spreading the food out thinly, so that it looks like a lot. But avoid talking about a diet. Our culture is overly obsessed with dieting, and this is not healthy. You need to establish healthy eating patterns in your child, not cyclical dieting patterns.

UNDERWEIGHT CHILD

I have a three-year-old son who is underweight. I have been given some suggestions by his pediatrician on how to get him to eat, but it's not working. Do you think I should just wait until he outgrows this, or is it something that will affect him later on? He will not eat meat or vegetables, other than potatoes.

When my children were small, I worried excessively over how much they should eat. When we moved from our first home when our oldest daughter was about five, I found a row of dried-up pieces of meat in some unused cupboards by our dining-room table. My daughter had chewed on them for a bit, decided she didn't like them, and put them aside! She was perfectly healthy, and the lack of those bits of meat had not hurt her. So, I began to understand that children will eat what they need. Mom needs to remember that God has put into each child a little biochemical computer. This computer tells that child over a period of weeks exactly how much food he needs and even what kinds of food he needs. Frankly, many eating problems are due to mothers' and fathers' anxiety and the power struggles that come from it. Here are some suggestions:

- Prepare simple, well-balanced meals that are attractive and tasty.

- Enjoy your own food and set an example for the child. Many children, in seeing the parents' enjoyment, will want to enjoy those foods.

- Give the child small amounts on his plate, allow him to eat all that he has, and then ask for seconds.

- Be sure at each meal to have at least one thing that the child likes, if possible. Most children love Jell-O with fruit, vegetable sticks, or pudding. These are all nourishing foods.

- Be sure that the meat is tender enough to chew (so the child won't have to hide it!).

- Keep snacks between meals small, so that your child will come to the table with a good appetite.

- Give him a muliple vitamin, and be patient. In due time your child will get all the food he needs.

BREAKING THE SWEETS HABIT

Unknown to us, our toddler was getting hooked on sweets, thanks to indulgent relatives and even church nursery workers. Now, at age three, she looks for candy or gum all of the time, from before breakfast until she is tucked into bed at night. I don't want to eliminate sweets, but how can we cut them down?

All parents face this difficulty of having to deny some things to their children, and certainly having too much sugary gum and candy is one of them. We know that the sugar in gum and candy promotes bacterial growth in the mouth which causes tooth decay. Gum can also cause choking in the very young.

Obviously there is one simple answer—sugarless gum. I have no strong objections to a child's chewing gum occasionally if it is sugar-free. Chewing, however, stimulates the flow of saliva from a child's mouth, which obviously must be swallowed, and that tends to stimulate the secretion of gastric juices. I have actually known children to have chronic stomachaches because their poor little tummies did not get enough rest due to chewing gum too much.

You can teach a child (of at least three) to gratify oral (sucking, chewing) needs just by eating proper foods, like raw vegetables. Younger toddlers and infants, however, should not have raw vegetables due to the danger of choking. Of course, gum tastes good, and it's fun in moderation—but use it as a special treat. It offers oral satisfaction without nutrition.

Explain to your daughter your concern about the problem with her having sweets or gum too much, so that she knows you are acting out of loving protection of her. Plan with her when she may and may not have candy or gum. Stick with that plan. Ask others not to treat her to sweets unless you okay it first. Be very firm, and follow through with your plan, allowing her to chew sugarless gum only when you and she agree that she may have it. Supply plenty of love and laughter, play and creativity, *and healthy food,* and your daughter will soon give up her fascination with sweets.

SERIOUS ILLNESS

How much should you tell a child who might be sick for a long time, or have some permanent disability from his illness, or who might even die?

Serious illness in a child is a brutal reality and one that I hope few of you will ever have to face. In working with chronically ill or critically ill children, there is a fine line between keeping hope alive to allow enjoyment of life, and being honest with the child.

In my experience, almost all seriously ill people have an inner sense about the severity of their illness. Children are no exception to this, and I do not recommend that you lie to your children or that you pretend that something is true which is overly optimistic.

What can you do, then, if you have a child who is seriously ill and potentially facing death? First, seek the physician's input. Get as many consultations as you need to be sure of the facts that you must communicate. Get help from your minister or a hospice worker to face the emotional and spiritual issues of that child's impending death or chronic illness. Talk together as mother and father, with relatives, and with friends, until you find the inner strength to communicate the facts to your child.

Then tell the child frankly and honestly, all of what you know about that illness. Give all the positives as well as the negatives and doubts. Offer the honest hope that is there, and teach the child to live each day to the fullest extent. Teach the child how to give to others in order to leave pleasant and happy memories with those who are left behind. Above all, teach that child faith in a heavenly Father who gives strength to cope and assurance of life after death.

HELP FOR EMOTIONALLY DISTURBED BOY

I have an eight-year-old son who is emotionally disturbed. Just recently, he was placed in a home for children with this kind of disorder. I'm hoping you can provide me with information that will enable me to cope with this situation when he finally does come home.

The most important guideline I can give to this mother of a troubled child is that she needs to avoid blaming herself or anyone else. She needs to avoid feeling guilty about the fact that her child has problems. Work through that as quickly as you can if you have a child with emotional disturbances.

Then be sure to believe, in fact *know,* that there is no shame in having such a problem. A great many people today still believe that an emotional disorder is an embarrassment and that parents and children should be ashamed of themselves! I would encourage you to give up such a belief (if you harbor it) and not tolerate it from other people.

Work hard to understand the reasons for your child's problems. Sometimes those problems come from misunderstandings or troubled communication within a family. You may have made mistakes in parenting, and you will need to make some changes in order to hasten your child's recovery and maintain it. Yet this does not mean you are to blame. I have rarely found parents who deliberately made parenting errors.

Sometimes physical illnesses or physical handicaps can contribute to emotional disturbances, so again there is a need to understand and not to blame yourselves.

Losses and grief that are beyond your control (or that of your child) are another reason for emotional disturbances.

Before your child returns, make any changes you need to to make family dynamics as healthy as possible. Find good medical and psychological resources to help you to guide him when he returns. Look for health and strength in your child more than illness, and learn to build on those strengths. Also find your own strengths. Nurture your faith in God and your child's faith. Ask for God to restore a loving, healthy relationship between you and your emotionally troubled child.

7

EDUCATION

EARLY LEARNING

Could you suggest what things I should be teaching my eleven-month-old baby? I'm referring to such things as colors, numbers, shapes, and words. I'm wondering how and when to teach and where to start.

This mother's question is startling, because this mother apparently feels she should be teaching academics to a baby. This child should be learning to feel safe; to feel warm and close; to laugh and love; and to find joy in life. The child is learning through sight, smell, hearing, taste, and touching. There should be a balance of physical activity along with cuddling, resting, and privacy. Children need the freedom to just *be,* to grow as God meant them to grow——and to be unconditionally accepted. When parents become anxious about teaching children, unconditional acceptance gets lost.

Early learning *is* possible. We know that little babies can learn a great many numerical concepts, but frankly I don't think that's desirable. For example, we have learned from studying children that those who learn how to read before school are no more advanced in their reading abilities by third grade than those who do not learn until the first grade. So I recommend that parents not try too hard to teach children academic skills before they start school.

PRESCHOOL: ESSENTIAL OR NOT?

My daughter hasn't been to nursery school, and I'm wondering if she'll be able to compete in kindergarten on an equal level with the kids who have already had some school experience. Do boys and girls who have been to nursery school have a head start over those who have not?

While the mother in the previous question was asking about her infant, this writer is asking about her preschooler. Preschool-age children can, indeed, benefit from skill training.

The following are the skills that preschoolers will benefit from having prior to kindergarten. Your child should pick up these skills at home if she does not get them through an organized preschool program.

Teach your child to interact socially by inviting children into your home or taking your child to a play group elsewhere. Sunday school and other church events also will give her the opportunity to interact with children her age.

Teach your preschooler the basic academic facts that she would learn in preschool. These facts include: basic colors such as red, yellow, blue, and green; recognizing letters and numbers from 1-10; following directions; being respectful and obedient; and, if possible, knowing her phone number and/or address.

Teach your preschooler to wait for and use the bathroom. Your child should know basic hygeine.

Teach her some basic physical skills such as throwing a ball, molding clay, swinging on a swing.

Help your child to learn to pay attention for about fifteen minutes at a time.

If you have enjoyed your child, and offered normal social interactions with similar-aged friends; if you've trained and disciplined her consistently, fairly, and lovingly; if you're proud of her and her potential for good, you need not fear any disadvantage for your preschool child when she enters kindergarten.

SCHOOL READINESS

Most parents probably have mixed emotions about waving good-bye on the first day of school. I'm looking forward to the new freedom, but I'm a little afraid that Jonathan isn't quite ready to face the world out there. Do you have any help for me?

When you're not sure if your child is ready, don't be afraid to ask other people. Check with a trusted relative, a Sunday-school teacher, or a professional in your school district. Many districts have a preschool screening that can help you to know whether your child is ready for kindergarten.

Boys tend to mature more slowly than girls, so it is more often boys with birthdays in the summer who are lacking in school readiness. If there is any serious question, allow your child to wait a year; I particularly recommend that for boys.

There are some specific signs that you can look for to help you know if your child is ready for school:

- Can your child hold a crayon and pencil and use them with reasonable success?
- Can your child dress himself and tie his shoelaces?

- Can he use the toilet alone satisfactorily?
- Can he share and take turns?
- Is he able to show respect for other children's feelings?
- Can he protect himself when that is necessary? or find help?
- Emotionally, can your child label some feelings?
- Is your child aware of his needs, and can he ask for what he needs?
- Is your child's attention span at least fifteen to twenty minutes long?

Read to your child. Deprive him of some television to spend time developing his motor skills and academic interests. Then send him off to school with joy and confidence.

READING-SKILL GROUPS

Do you think it is a good idea to divide a class up by reading skills?

If you can remember back as far as first grade, you may recall being placed in reading groups based on level of skill. I have worked with school districts for a number of years, and I have debated in my own mind the pros and cons of this issue.

We need to think about what happens to a classroom of students when the slower readers are placed with the gifted readers. The less-gifted child is quickly going to run the risk of feeling that there is no hope for him. *This child is doing well, so I must be dumb* is how some children react, so teachers separate them to ensure they won't compare themselves.

On the other hand, putting children into different groups still singles them out as being different because they are in a particular group. Children can quickly attach a value to a certain group.

What is important to a child's success in school, as well as at home, is the acceptance of that child for who he or she is. Every child has some gifts and special abilities that are unique to him or her, and those assets are the important points for teachers and parents to understand and value.

READING TO CHILDREN

At what ages do children really benefit from and enjoy having their parents read to them?

Any age! One of the most pleasant ways for a parent and child to spend time together is in the sharing of a good book.

Some parents fail to think about reading to older children. Since the advent of the television, VCRs, video games, and computers, children have become so electronically entertained that reading to one another (or sometimes even conversing with one another) has become a lost art. The benefits of reading are so many that I would really like to list them:

- Reading together produces a sense of intimacy.
- Reading together teaches the value of reading.
- Reading together builds vocabulary.
- Reading a good book teaches good values.
- Reading together enriches a child's reading experience because he can listen to books that would be too difficult for him to read on his own.
- Reading together exposes children to a wider variety of literature than they might pick on their own.
- Reading allows the child and parent to share a rich experience together—to travel to foreign lands, to long-ago or future times, to overcome danger and solve mysteries.

I wish for you real joy and warmth as you and your child share books.

PARENTS AS TALENT SCOUTS

How can parents go about uncovering their child's talents?

Parents need to be talent scouts. They must explore as many areas of their children's lives as possible to see where their talents lie. Here are some areas to check out:

1. Culture: Help your child explore art and music, literature, and photography. Share with your child your own interest in these areas of life.

2. Sports and athletics: Expose your child to gymnastics, swimming, running, skating, skiing, tennis, soccer, football, baseball, basketball, or any other sports that you can think of. Not only does this develop your child's skills, but you may discover with your child some special area of skill that could become a lifelong joy or a professional ability.

3. Nature: Children need to learn from and about nature. Sitting and listening, or walking through woods or across beaches can give you the opportunity to teach your child the joy of nature. You may find your child has a special interest in ecology, gardening, or taking care of animals.

4. Science: Children can do a lot of experiments in their own homes that will introduce them to the wonders of physics, chemistry, biology, and astronomy. Children's museums in many areas also allow opportunities for children to do hands-on science. You may find you have a budding nuclear physicist, lab technician, physician, rock collector, or meteorologist in your house.

5. History: Local museums offer lots of opportunities for learning about local and regional history. If you travel to other parts of the country, you can study history there, also. You may find that your child has a yen to learn about other cultures or to collect old coins or other mementos.

6. Making things: Don't overlook a child's interest or gift-edness in building, cooking, gardening, or other hands-on activities. There are many industries and service trades that allow people to work with their hands.

7. Serving others: See if your child might enjoy helping at a soup kitchen or homeless shelter. A desire to help others might lead to a career in the healthcare, mental health, or social service.

Exploring does not mean that you try to make your child become a master at every area mentioned here. Let these times of exploring be superficial at first. Take a look, dip into the various areas of interest, and let your child have fun with them. It is out of this simple exploration that the commitment to a life career will eventually be made, but probably not for many years. In the meantime, help your child find at least one area that she is interested in and help her to excel in that area, whether it's music or stamp collecting, biking or gardening. Praise the results of her projects, and she will be likely to explore more deeply on her own.

DETECTING LEARNING DISABILITIES

What are some of the symptoms a child might manifest if he had a learning disability?

Those are fairly easy to define in some cases. The most common disability is learning and language disability. For example, problems with reversing letters and simple words. A *b* for example to a child with learning disabilities looks like a *d*, a *q* may look like a *g*. A simple word such as *dab* becomes *bad* to a child with a learning disability. Now that sort of learning disability can be helped simply by requiring the child to memorize by practicing again and again the right shape and the right name for that letter.

However, in many children the process and the problem of

a learning disability is much more complex than that. In some children there is a difficulty in translating what the eyes see into a concept that the cortex or the outer layer of the brain can interpret. The same is true of the hearing; what a child hears simply may not get from all of those complex nerve tracts in the brain to be interpreted into something that is meaningful to a child. Such children have difficulty with what we call short-term memory. They have trouble seeing or hearing something, and remembering, even for a few minutes, what is going on. They may remember what happened last week or last year, but not what happened a few seconds ago. They often intensely dislike reading, spelling, and writing assignments, or math. Word comprehension may be poor, and the child might have difficulty sounding out new words.

The technical terms associated with learning disorders include Auditory Discrimination Defect, Expressive Language Disorder, Reading Disorder, Mathematics Disorder, and so on. These are simply descriptive terms relating to how a child learns. None of these means that your child lacks abilities. They just mean he will have some difficulty in learning.

Another area associated with learning disabilities is Attention Deficit Disorder (ADD or ADHD). Children who suffer from this are usually impulsive, forgetful, disorganized, and cannot concentrate for more than a few minutes at a time. Some have little ability to empathize and thus have difficulty making and keeping friends. Those with hyperactivity are difficult to be around due to their fidgeting, squirming, and physical destructiveness. Intensive, consistent discipline along with controlling the child's environment (especially in the classroom) can have a tremendously positive effect on children with ADD. There are also several excellent medications that greatly help in relieving these symptoms.

A final type of school difficulty or learning disability has to do with emotional problems. Depression or anxiety about school or about problems at home can cause impairment in a child's learning which mimic learning disabilities.

The causes of learning problems are numerous. Of course, neurological weaknesses might be due to birth defects or some problem even before birth. It may be an inherited or genetic problem. Children become discouraged through their own failures or through seeing other children get ahead of them. They may compensate by becoming the class clown or acting out in various antisocial ways.

Special classes and special learning techniques can help many children overcome learning disabilities. Have your little child build letters out of blocks or string, or something that he can feel and touch while he is creating the letter. Repeat the sound of the letter as he builds it, while he is learning. Keep the child's mind free from worry by explaining the events of his life and assuming adult responsibility for the child so that he does not need to carry them. Praise your child's successes, and discipline him so he can become responsible. He will learn to succeed if you are patient and loving.

CAN'T READ?

My son can't read. He has been through four years of learning-disability programs and has been to five different schools. We are confused and very concerned. He's been living with his dad until this year, and now he's living with me and my new husband. In a few weeks I'm going to start working half days so that I can help him more and build a closer bond between us.

This mother has a legitimate concern. Her child clearly is old enough that he should be reading by now, even if his reading were delayed somewhat. Since he has been through several learning-disability (LD) programs, I would assume that a variety of methods have been tried. However, I think this mother's decision to spend time with him herself may be a very good one.

I would recommend that this mother speak with the LD resource person at her son's current school to obtain recommendations on how she can work with him at home in a way that will complement what is being done in school. Then, she should spend limited amounts of time with him at home working on reading. Chances are that he will not be able to tolerate more than one or two thirty-minute sessions of work on reading a few times per week. She should be sure that he is trying to read material that is interesting to him. Take him to the library and let him select what he wants to read.

She should also spend time reading to him, as that will allow him to discover the world of great literature even though he is not a great reader himself. Perhaps he would enjoy some of the old classics of adventure literature such as *Treasure Island* or *Robinson Crusoe,* which are available in abridged form for children. Or perhaps he needs more modern stories, like space adventures or detective mysteries.

I notice that this child has had a fair amount of upheaval in his life of late. He has changed schools five times, has been through a divorce, and has just changed homes. He needs some stability and a lot of unconditional love and acceptance. As his life settles down and his self-esteem builds through loving contact with his parents, perhaps his reading will slowly advance. If not, the mother should continue seeking help through the professionals in her school district and perhaps her pediatrician to find a solution for this child's problem.

REPEATING A GRADE

What questions should parents ask if their child's school recommends that he repeat a grade?

I have a list of questions that should be considered in deciding such an important issue. Whether to hold a child back is a difficult decision, and parents need to give it careful consideration.

My first question is this: *How does his age and physical size fit with the other children in his present grade and in the grade that he would be in if he were held back?* If he is a great deal bigger or feels older than the class he would be in, he may resent it and rebel, so holding him back would not be effective.

The second question: *How badly are his academic skills lacking?* Is the lack apparent in all areas of learning or only in one or two special areas? (If he is lacking in only one or two special areas, perhaps tutoring could help him improve.)

The third question: *What are his social skills?* If he is quite mature, he may feel out of place with younger children. If he is less mature, he may feel better with the younger ones, and that would help his adjustment.

The fourth question: *What are the other choices?* Are there special classes? Is there a teacher who may be good with children like him?

These choices can help you decide wisely what is best for your child. If all of the answers say, "This child is not mature enough; he needs strengthening in all of his learning," then he may need to repeat a grade.

PARENTS OF A REPEATING CHILD

Our daughter has been recommended to repeat second grade. We agree with the recommendation, because she has always been the youngest in the class because of her August birthday. She was also born prematurely and has lagged a little behind her peers in terms of maturity. But we are having trouble dealing with our feelings about this recommendation.

Such a decision can be very tough on all concerned. Here's what how you can deal with this:

1. Parents need to face their sadness. All parents have dreams and ideals for their children, and repeating a grade rarely fits into those dreams. When your dream is lost (or you think it might be) you have to grieve, so do your grieving, and then accept the fact. When you have grieved through the loss, and you have accepted it, then you will be ready to help your child go through the same process.

2. Allow the child to grieve also. Most children are sad if they have to repeat a grade because they lose the social contacts they have built through the years.

3. Explore the advantages of repeating this grade. Help her to see how fortifying her educational foundation will help her for the rest of her school life. Keep your attitude positive, and it will help your child to stay positive as well. Work closely with the school, and make next year the best year your child will have. Facing disappointments, overcoming them, and moving on—that's what you and your child can learn even if she must repeat a grade.

CREATIVITY

Are some people born with more creativity? Or is it something that's developed?

Your child may not grow up to be Beethoven, Cassatt, or Michelangelo, but no matter what occupation she chooses, she will benefit from learning to think creatively. I believe that everyone is made in the likeness of God and therefore is creative. Each person, however, is born with different potential and possibly a different area for the expression of that creativity. Though some kids are born with creative gifts or have a genetic factor that makes them follow a certain path, they can also be taught the excitement of creative thinking by their enthusiastic parents.

Look for your child's areas of interest and skill. What excites her? Much creativity depends on the parents' encouraging and providing opportunities for that interest to be developed in the child. Whatever the child creates demands recognition and praise.

MUSIC LESSONS

Could you discuss some of the factors parents should think about if they are considering music lessons for their child?

Recent research has indicated that music lessons can be generally beneficial to children, helping them to achieve more, especially in the areas of science and math. Thus, media attention has shone on music lessons as a way to enhance a child's learning. Parents naturally want their child to have the best and fullest life possible, and to some moms and dads that includes lessons. I think the very first thing that parents need to consider is whether they are willing to commit themselves to the agony as well as the ecstasy of such learning.

There are about three phases that children go through in learning any special skill. Usually the first stage is that of *excitement* at the new opportunity. The opportunity to touch those keys and learn what those funny little black notes mean is usually very intriguing. This can be fairly short-lived, however, and the second phase is one of *boredom and resistance* to the monotony of scales and practicing. Once a child gets through that difficult stage, however, she can then know the *thrill of mastery.* Somewhere in the process, children may hit a time of severe discouragement if they find they are not making progress as quickly as hoped. That may or may not happen to your child.

When considering whether to enroll your child in music lessons, first *evaluate your child's natural gifts.* I think all children need to learn and appreciate music, because music has been called the universal language. If your child does begin lessons, try to *avoid rigidity and negativism.* If your child continues past the honeymoon stage, *don't let him quit during that resistant phase.* Set up a plan (with your child's cooperation and perhaps with advice from the teacher) in these ways:

1. Keep practice time short enough to be bearable.

2. Keep the practice time frequent enough to learn the lesson. Fifteen minutes of practice six days per week is far better than trying to cram an hour or more of practice into the day before the lesson.

3. Encourage a time to play the instrument just for fun, without the hard work of practicing.

4. Try playing the instrument yourself. Having your child teach you something about it can captivate his interest and promote his real work and effort in finding the mastery that can be such a thrill—such an advantage in his life.

5. Ask your teacher for fun ways to practice. Children can "go fishing" (with a stick and string and magnet) for fish (paper fish with paper clips) that have the names of the pieces they should play; they can go on a hunt that takes them through their repertoire ("Play 'Hunter's Chorus' and then go check the TV"; and on the TV is a note: "Play a scale and then . . . "); or they can have a friend over and practice together. There are many ways to make practicing fun. Ask at a large music store for suggestions on where to find these ideas.

6. If your child, his teacher, and you feel that his progress is slow due to lack of interest, then allow him to quit if he wants to.

CHRISTIAN SCHOOL?

Do you think a child should be put in a Christian

school if at all possible, or should he be allowed to remain in the public school?

Many parents today are looking for alternatives to public education. And, while there are many such alternatives that work very well, I have also seen families trade off great creativity and richness in the public school for a restrictive attitude and lack of equipment in a private school. Therefore, there are several requirements that I suggest you look for if you are seeking a Christian school for your child.

First, you need to find out if there is a balance in the academic, physical, social, and cultural teachings of that school, as well as the spiritual teachings. The former should not be sacrificed in the interests of spiritual education.

Second, look for genuine warmth and openness, unconditional acceptance of each child as he is, structure and discipline, and the kind of guidance that helps him to achieve and grow. Look for a friendliness among the staff, and especially between the faculty and students. The lives of your children will be influenced by those teachers. Avoid a school that feels like a reformatory, with rigid expectations and acceptance based only on performance. Some parents use private schools to reform children who have not done well in public school, but this emphasis on discipline can be easily overdone.

Third, I would search for a general flavor of excellence in the school, an environment that is clean and neat, with adequate equipment in computer centers and science labs, as well as academic teaching that is creative, challenging, and geared to the child's growth. Also look at the number and kind of extra-curricular activities.

Remember parents, even if you send your child to a Christian school, it is you who hold the responsibility for teaching your faith to your children. Your example becomes the most convincing teacher. The activities you share, the compassion you show, the generosity you practice, the conversations you hold—all teach your children how to live and how to walk daily with God.

HOME SCHOOL

What are the advantages and the disadvantages of teaching your child at home rather than sending him off to school?

There is a growing home-school movement that encourages parents to teach their children, following a set curriculum, rather than send them to public schools. This option is attractive to many parents who harbor concerns about the public schools: e.g., overcrowded classrooms, the lack of special programs for exceptional children, the possibly negative influence of peers, the acquisition of bad manners, the influence of non-Christian teachers, and the impact of non-Christian philosophies in some textbooks.

I share these worries about public schools, but I also have concerns that some people may choose to home school who are not equipped to handle its demands. I personally cannot think of more than 5 percent of my acquaintances whom I would consider up to the task of home schooling.

Many parents cannot handle the constant interaction with children that such a plan would require. They have to fulfill a dual role. Shifting gears from parent to teacher and back can be draining on both parents and children. Providing constant supervision, yet finding the energy to enjoy the child and relax and play together, is difficult, if not impossible, for some. Further, some parents are not educationally equipped to handle all the material that children must master. Parents with little background in science and math, for example, may struggle to teach children these subjects in upper grades.

Home schooling often takes place in the elementary grades

with children going back to public school in the later grades. In elementary school, children are very open to their parents' influence and will readily accept a parental view of the culture around them. But in secondary school, the children are much more influenced by peers, and so the transition from home school to secondary school can be quite jarring at a vulnerable time in the child's life.

So, home schooling certainly has its advantages, but it is not something to be taken on without much thought and consideration. In the end, you must choose whether you will try this for your child.

TROUBLE IN SCHOOL

We know that every child has a need to feel wanted and liked in school. Our son has a problem in this area. He goes to a lot of trouble to make his classmates notice him. If another child hits him, he'll turn and do the same. He is in trouble often. He does have some friends, but his attitude toward school is very poor and is getting worse.

This sounds like a child who is insecure and needs help. It must be understood that every person needs attention. That's simply universal. A child prefers a positive, happy kind of attention, but if he doesn't get enough of that, he will settle for just being noticed, even in negative ways. Children who have moved a lot sometimes get into this pattern. They may have trouble facing the repeated loss of friends and familiar places. Further, the absence of a parent may cause insecurity. Boys and girls benefit from having two parents involved in their lives. If one or both parents are unavailable due to work responsibilities, health issues, or geographical or emotional distance, then a child will struggle to feel valued.

Stop feeling sorry for your child if he is not getting along well in school. Refuse to rescue him from the consequences of his misbehaviors, because sooner or later his friends and teachers will help him to learn that he must behave more considerately. Find your son's assets, interests, and talents. Develop and encourage them, and help him to feel proud of himself.

You also might consider checking to see if your child is hyperactive. I have discovered that many students who develop problems like these have Attention Deficit Disorder. They are impulsive and insensitive to others. Sometimes they compensate for difficulties in class by making trouble outside of school. If you suspect ADD, have your child evaluated by a pediatrician or psychiatrist. Disciplinary systems and medication can help greatly.

Meanwhile, teach your child social skills at home. Help him learn to take turns, be a good sport, and resolve conflict without violence. And praise him when he does well.

8

EMOTIONAL DEVELOPMENT

HOME ENVIRONMENT

If you were to describe the perfect home environment for children to grow and develop, what factors would be most important?

What a wonderful question! Here's what I would advise:

1. Work on the marriage. Having two parents who respect and love each other is a major positive factor in children's lives. Parents, be sure that you communicate respect for one another in front of your children. Love is wonderful, but it is not very helpful unless it is communicated clearly, consistently, and honestly.

2. Give unconditional, loving acceptance. Accepting each child for exactly who he or she is constitutes another essential factor in a secure family life. Approval and disapproval must be communicated in a positive fashion, so that support, encouragement, and cooperation are common.

3. Offer appropriate correction and discipline. These are essential for children to grow in their self-awareness, in interacting successfully with other people, and in learning a sense of compassion for others.

4. Provide a congenial atmosphere. Make wholesome laughter common in your household. Be careful, however, that your laughter is never ridicule of someone else.

5. Involve extended family. One of the most secure things in my childhood was my extended family. My grandmother lived with us until I was a senior in high school, when she quietly passed away. Her presence was an influential factor in my life. The uncles, aunts, and cousins that surrounded us also were comforting in times of illness or distress. Helping your child to know your extended family can require special planning in today's mobile society. But telephone calls, letters, and visits can give your children that sense of being a part of generations. The extended family will help them to feel the security of belonging to something larger than themselves.

Not all extended families are positive influences, however. Some family members are negative, overly critical, judgmental, or even abusive or alcoholic. If this is the case, then the children will not benefit from frequent exposure to these family members. Instead, help your children to love these family members, to enjoy the good in them, and to recognize their failures in order to avoid repeating them.

6. Show hospitality. Make your home a welcoming place for your children's friends. This will be a springboard for their becoming healthy adults and a place for returning when they need a shelter as they grow older.

HUGGING YOUR CHILD

Do children ever outgrow the need for hugging and cuddling from their parents?

All of us, including adults, need hugging and touching, so I really think children never grow out of that. However, they certainly do go through stages in which they would make parents believe they do not need cuddling. But even in those difficult stages of the establishment of their own identity, children still need touching. They simply need it in private, and they need it in different ways. Find the time of day at which children are the most accessible to stroking or touching. It is often at bedtime. Make the rounds to each child. Try a variety of touches—a back rub, scratching the head, stroking the forehead, or a little tickling may be acceptable at times. Sit by the bedside, talk awhile, try some sort of touch, then give them a kiss as you leave.

We need to understand that when a child seems to reject touch, it is a normal part of growing up. Do not take it as a personal rejection. As you stay patient and understanding, and remain available to your child emotionally, the warmth and the hugs will come and go. But the security remains.

PRIVACY

What guidelines would you offer parents on the subject of children's privacy?

There are three major factors that I think can help parents understand the need for privacy and how it changes with age. One is the *age of the child.* The second is *the child's personality,* and the third is the *mood or the circumstance of the moment.*

Age. Prior to the age of six or seven, children rarely need privacy. Up to three or four years of age, a child needs to always be within sight or hearing of an adult. But after age six or seven, a child begins to need some time alone in order to become an independent individual. By the age of ten or eleven, a child's needs for privacy increase greatly and they continue increasing through the teenage years.

Personality. Some children are extroverts and need and want very little privacy. On the other hand, the introverted child enjoys and needs much more time alone.

Mood or circumstances. Privacy needs also relate directly to the current circumstances and mood of the child. Some children, when hurt or angry, want attention, hugs, and comfort from their parents. But others need their "space." They need time to cool down and figure out their emotions a little bit. Such children demand parental ingenuity and sensitivity. Recognizing and respecting the child's need for time to think through anger or hurt is very important. Later on, you can go to the child's room and knock on the door and see if your child is ready for a hug or a talk. If not, keep returning at intervals until she or he is ready.

OVERPROTECTION

How can parents keep from being overprotective of their children?

Recently I worked with a third-grade girl in a public school. She took tiny baby steps when she walked. She talked in a babyish tone of voice and used a little child's vocabulary. Though she was very bright, she was unable to fit in with the other children and was afraid to play in their active games. She was an insecure, unhappy child who cried a great deal. As we explored the reasons for this child's difficulty at school, we found that the mother had really enjoyed her daughter as a baby and had unwittingly kept her child small, overprotected, and babyish, giving herself a little baby for a long time, but creating in her daughter a serious problem as she grew.

Here are some ideas to consider if you think you are being overprotective:

- recognize your child's strengths and help her use them
- believe in your own good parenting skills
- understand that your purpose is to guide your child *to* independence
- by using careful questions, help your child make good decisions and stick to them
- let her know that you believe in her
- maintain an affirming attitude

I find that oftentimes overprotective parents are those who either were raised by overprotective parents or, on the other extreme, were neglected. In other cases, serious illness or accidents cause parents to overprotect a child in an attempt to prevent such a problem from recurring. Whatever the cause, you can be a protective parent without being overprotective.

CHILDREN'S MEMORY BANK

My friend, who is studying psychology, says she learned that children store all they see and hear, even if they don't readily understand or use the information. This bothers me, mostly because my husband and I have gotten angry and yelled at our daughters at times. What effect does this have and how can we reconcile these times with them?

Children do indeed record experiences, good and bad. But children especially tend to remember the things that are emotionally charged, either a very happy time or, unfortunately, something that is painful. However, being angry and yelling are things most parents do, so I would not go off on a heavy guilt trip. When your anger is aimed at correcting your children's problems, and love prompts that anger, then you need not be overly concerned. If you are in doubt about how your children feel about their past, ask them. They will usually be very quick to tell you.

It is important, nonetheless, that you learn to correct your children *without* intense anger. Extreme anger eventually can cause fear and then rebellion. Learn to give yourself a bit of a "timeout." Use it to think about whatever lesson your child needs to learn in a given situation. Consider how you can teach it most effectively (e.g., calm, firm, limit setting and consequences). Then put your plan into action.

A picture that is a masterpiece always has contrasts in it. It takes the dark and the light, the bright and the faded colors, to make a picture really beautiful. And in molding the lives of your children, you are creating a masterpiece. It takes sadness, anger, joy, and peace to make those lives balanced and to teach your children the concept of reality. In talking with your children from time to time, it is helpful to review the past. Remind them of events from early childhood—times that they have probably forgotten. In telling those stories, you will have a wonderful opportunity to interpret the past for them, giving them reasons for the things that happened. They will know then that it was love that prompted discipline.

TEACHING LOVE

Other than through the parent's basic care and feeding, how does a child learn about love?

Love is taught by loving parents—parents who love each other, who love themselves, who love the baby, and who love God. The warm exuberance over the presence of a baby is the presence of love. Love is not only caught, however, it is also taught, and the teaching of love is essential for parents to understand. The tender care for the needs of a baby or an older child are equally important in keeping love alive in the life of that child. Love is taught by using a gentle, loving tone of voice rather than a harsh, angry, yelling voice. Love is also taught by saying loving and positive words to a child, encouraging that child rather than scolding, lecturing, or putting her down. She will see love in your eyes, hear it in your voice, feel it in your touch, and know it by your total care.

CAUSE OF NIGHTMARES

My grandson, who's four and a half years old, has nightmares. He also cries often during the day, but not as much as he once did.

Children's nightmares certainly are disturbing, not only to the child, but to the parents as well. I find that when children and parents do not get their sleep, the fatigue factor causes a great deal of stress within the family. Actually, in most cases nightmares themselves are caused by too much stress. Sometimes that's because expectations are too high. (I find that many times children in school who are struggling for grades have nightmares.) Punishment that is too severe, or consequences that are administered with too much anger can cause problems in a child's life that may come out through bad dreams. Stress in peer relationships or stress caused by the child's own perceptions of things can also cause nightmares.

In addition, illness as well as certain physical conditions contribute to nightmares. Children who have difficulty breathing because of nasal allergies or asthma may have sleep disturbances. Inconsistencies on the parents' or teachers' behalf can create anxiety and nervousness, and the child dreams those out in nightmares.

At the other end of the spectrum, sometimes too much freedom can cause anxiety. Many preschoolers have a great deal of freedom to roam geographically about the neighborhood, as well as much emotional freedom and little closeness within the family. Children need to have a great deal of cuddling and physical closeness, as well as emotional intimacy and warmth, if they are to be secure enough so that they won't have nightmares. Balancing your child's freedom and supervision is important.

Frightening experiences that children see or hear about can also cause nightmares. Television programs or news items discussed around the table at dinner can register in a little child's mind in a frightening fashion.

Of course, nightmares are not all bad. Dreams do help children to get rid of some of their fears, but a vicious cycle can develop if the dreams begin terrifying the child. Some children dread going to bed at night for fear of their recurrent nightmares.

The cure for nightmares really is fairly simple, once you understand the causes. Simply *decrease the stress in your child's life*. Make sure you provide that fine balance between freedom and expectations, and lessen the severity of your punishments if you think that is a contributing factor. Speak with his playmates' parents and other who might be able to tell you if anything frightening or upsetting has happened.

Give lots of unconditional love. Spend more time with the child, particularly in the evening, reading stories, cuddling, and playing happy games, allowing your child to go to bed feeling confident, warm, and secure. I recommend leaving a nightlight on; eliminate any frightening things from the room, such as pictures or shadows that might look scary at night. Surround your child with a sense of protection, and you will not spoil him. You will be offering him the security he needs to grow up happily.

CHILDHOOD GRIEF

My husband and I have two sons, three and a half years and eighteen months old. We recently had a baby who was stillborn. Our oldest son was truly excited about the new baby. He had felt the baby's movements and heard the heartbeat while in the womb. The loss of the baby had many effects on him. He has begun wetting his pants, sleeping and eating poorly, and behaving unpredictably and rebelliously.

This certainly is a family crisis. Death is the ultimate loss with all of the helplessness and sadness it causes in the survivors. It's very difficult for adults to deal with death and can be more difficult for children. The stages of grief, as formulated by Elisabeth Kübler-Ross and others, are important to review briefly: First, there is denial that it has actually happened, then a sense of loss, anger over that loss, and finally, preoccupation with sadness, pain, fear, and guilt, that go along with all grief. Eventually, however, healing does come!

A child facing a family member's death will probably experience fear as well—fear of the adults' grief and his own pain; fear that possibly this death is a punishment for some of his naughtiness; fear that he might die if another child could die. A child certainly is going to feel angry, and this anger covers up his pain and fear. His rebellious behavior is simply acting out the anger he feels. The following steps are recommended to help a child deal with grief:

First, *explain as much as you can.* Help the child understand that it is not his fault. You don't have to defend God and try to make the death look okay, either, because at this time the child is not going to believe that or feel it.

Second, *be honest.* Admit that you do not have all the answers to the child's feelings or even your own at this time.

Third, *be reassuring.* Make sure your child knows you love and accept him, even in the midst of his regressive and unpleasant behaviors. Baby him a great deal and give him the comfort of your physical presence frequently.

Fourth, *encourage emotional expression in appropriate forms.* Help him to put his fear and anger and guilt into words, if possible, or to express them on a pounding board or in tears. Cry with him, if you feel like it, and comfort him.

And yes, *allow your child to participate in the visitation and/or the funeral.* I recommend that children attend the funeral home and view the casket and the body, if possible. The ceremony of a funeral is one way of expressing grief. Being there to see the person who has died and knowing where the body is helps us all to complete that grief process in a concrete way. Also, more and more funeral homes are putting together special programs for children who are grieving. Check with your local homes.

Grief and loss are facts of life. You and your child can and must learn to cope with and transcend it together.

PARENT-CHILD DIFFERENCES

What kinds of family problems grow out of personality differences between a parent and child?

A great many problems can develop. A pediatrician in New York City a number of decades ago began studying parents and children from birth. She followed as many as possible for a number of years, and her discoveries are worth thinking about. She found, for example, that when a mother who was placid and loved peace and quiet had a child who was energetic and into everything, she developed a problem with that child almost from birth. Resentments began to grow between them that became lifelong and serious in their impact. On the contrary, she found that a mother who was energetic and active might have a child who was very peaceful, quiet, and introverted. She could become impatient and troubled about such a child, and set the stage for discrepancies and resentments that create disharmony in the family.

I find many times that parents love to cuddle babies, and yet some babies don't like to be cuddled. They squirm or stiffen and simply will not relax and settle into the mother's arms. That can cause resentment. A mother may fear that somehow there is something wrong with her as the mother or that the baby doesn't love her. Unconsciously, animosity and power struggles may grow that will set up the parent and child for serious problems later on. One mother spent her years of motherhood feeling cheated because she did not have a child with the temperament of her dreams!

Here are some simple rules for living in harmony as a family: *Define your unpleasant feelings toward your child.* Whom does she look like, or what is it that she does that creates problems for you? Make peace with the person she reminds you of (or work on your anger and grief if the child reminds you of your former spouse), and reconcile yourself to those traits as a gift of God to your child.

Then, *learn to accept and love her as she is.* Unconditionally, give that child the attention and the love that she needs in the way that she can best accept. As you affirm your child, you will build up some hope for her worth and success. You will see that child bloom, and you and your child will grow together.

ACCEPTING VS. EXPECTING

Isn't it a good thing for parents to have dreams and ambitions for their children?

Whether consciously or unconsciously, most of us as parents

have dreams for our children. Some of these hopes and dreams are for opportunities we ourselves missed when we were growing up. Or sometimes we want our children to experience exciting and happy times like those we had in the past. But whatever the source of our dreams, we need to be careful that they do not become an unbearable burden for our children, because serious problems can result.

I have known fathers who wanted their boys to become great, muscular football players, yet they had little boys who would have been crushed on any football field. Other parents wanted a girl who would be a cheerleader or the homecoming queen. They implicitly communicate to their daughter that she will never quite measure up unless she is a cheerleader.

Therefore, parents can eliminate disappointment over impossible dreams by adapting themselves to reality and looking towards dreams that match the child's gifts and interests. Every child has special gifts, and the parents' dream should be that of helping the child discover those unique, individual abilities and talents, and then valuing the ones the child has.

FAMILY TRAUMA AND PARENTAL VISITATION

In a family where I baby-sit there was recently a divorce. There are two children, a two-year-old and a four-year-old, but I'm writing mostly about the older boy. He has constant nightmares about his mother. She was abusive and beat him when he was younger. Now she has visiting rights for an hour a month, but the four-year-old does not want to see her. He has kicking and screaming fits when he goes and is difficult to deal with both before and after the visit.

With the prevalence of child abuse today, a great many families must cope with this kind of situation. Children must have protection and reassurance, and this child particularly needs to know that his mother will never hurt him again. It might help this child if he were shown on a watch or a clock just how long an hour is. If he knows when the time is up and that he'll get to leave at that time, he is likely to feel a little more secure and less frightened. If the visits are not supervised, perhaps they should be to ensure that the mother is not terrorizing the child during that brief visit. And if the situation continues, the child should be given the option to refuse the visits. He needs to feel that he has some control over the situation, since he undoubtedly felt powerless when his mother was abusing him.

As this child grows, I would recommend that his father teach him about his mother. Some background information (without gruesome details if she was abused) might help the child to understand why his mother acts the way she does. It will also confirm that his being a bad boy was never the cause of her rage.

Although this may sound odd, it might be wise to give the child a wildflower or a small gift to take when he has a visit with Mom. Children like to give gifts and it often empowers them to do so. And empowerment (or a sense of control) is exactly what this child needs. Also, it may help his mother to view the child more lovingly. Despite the abuse, she probably wants to see her child and in her own way she loves him.

The father and the baby-sitter need to invite the child to talk out his fears—past, present, and future. Verbalizing his anger, as well as his fears, can help to relieve the pressure and tension within him, and enable him to get over the tragedy of his past.

This child is perhaps fortunate to be having nightmares, because we believe that through dreams and nightmares some of our fears are released. I recommend that the father or the baby-sitter take this child into their arms when he awakens at night. Comfort him, awaken him if possible, and get him to talk about what he has been dreaming. Reassure him before putting him back to bed, and then at a later time talk about the dream, reassuring him that he will not have to worry about those fears anymore. Comfort and reassurance, encouragement and love—these are the qualities that will heal the hurts of this child's life.

9

DISCIPLINE AND TRAINING

INCONSISTENCY

How can my husband and I avoid being inconsistent in disciplining our children when we don't always agree on what our family rules should be? How will inconsistency affect our children?

Predictability is one of the basic emotional needs that all children have. But you cannot be consistent as parents until you are reasonably united. *That's* where you need to start. Talk and negotiate until you do come to an agreement. If that demands the outside help of a counselor, don't be afraid to seek that help. At least in your basic policies you must be in agreement. The best results in child rearing involve clear, reasonable, and meaningful guidelines enforced consistently, day after day.

When the disagreement involves minor matters, it's quite all right to let your discussions teach your child how to be honest and to disagree lovingly and discuss constructively in order to reach a successful compromise. In major matters, however, such disagreements create a climate for manipulation. I know one family in which the daughter has learned repeatedly to go to her father for things that she wants, because he is a softer touch than her mother. That has created resentment, guilt, and fear among the members of that family.

Here are some simple guidelines, that will help spouses in establishing consistency with your family. First, *identify goals* that you want to reach for and with your children. How do you want her to behave? What do you want her to achieve in life? When you think about those goals, it will draw you together, because there is no question that both moms and dads want the very best for each of their children.

Once you have set those goals, *plan the methods for reaching them.* That demands that you establish some basic policies and rules for your family. It also implies that there must be teaching and modeling of the qualities and values that you are talking about. Decide which parent can best enforce each rule. In some cases, the mother may be far more effective, and in others the father may be. Each one must take the lead in their best areas, *but back one another up in a consistent, united fashion.* Working for consistency is not an easy task. It will be well worth the struggle.

SPANKING

Many child specialists recommend that parents not spank children. But others say this is permissive and that children should be spanked. What do you think?

Many years ago I began to realize that even the most loving parents, under enough stress, can cross the line from punishment to abuse. This has prompted me to rethink my attitudes towards spanking.

Advocates of spanking quote the old proverb (Proverbs 13:24; 22:15 and others) about sparing the rod and spoiling the child. I always believe the wisdom of God's Word. And God's Word talks about the rod and staff of a shepherd. Let's look at what that means.

As a girl, I often tended my father's sheep. If they strayed into the wrong pastures, they could die. My job was to stay constantly alert. If one sheep headed for the wrong pasture, I would gently prod him with a stick. It took relatively little poking to get him back where he belonged. A beating not only failed to work, but it often created anger and could draw an attack.

In my five decades of work with children, I have rarely, if ever, seen this philosophy fail: Parents must stay watchful at all times and firmly and lovingly guide their kids into safe pastures.

If you are considering spanking a child, ask yourself:

1. What do I want my child to learn about life and avoiding errors? (In other words, what is the point I'm trying to make? Will it be made by a spanking?)

2. What is the *least* painful consequence that will teach these lessons? (Strict parents often err on the side of overpunishing a child. In general, a little punishment goes a long way.)

3. How can I follow through with consistent guidance?

I think that you will find that gentle, firm restraint, timeouts, and the loss of cherished privileges, along with your appropriate disapproval and boundary tending, will eliminate the need for spankings.

HOW TO AVOID SPANKING

Our son is almost four years old, and we're trying to use spanking less often as a form of punishment because we were spanking him almost every day. But

we're having a hard time getting away from spanking, because that seems to be all he'll respond to.

Spanking does, of course, allow for the alleviation of guilt through suffering pain over one's misdeed. Often, however, spankings do not stop or change the pattern of a child's misbehavior. They simply allow the child to feel free to misbehave again!

My parents were very strict people. My father was the authority in our family, and obedience was demanded. However, I can recall only two spankings in my entire life. When I hear of a child who is getting spanked every day, I feel sad, because I know there is a great deal of tension and ill will in that family.

In good discipline the parent must be creative. One time my father got me up late at night to go outside in the cold and darkness to do a chore I should have done when it was lighter and warmer. That taught me a very important lesson. He did not lay a hand on me, but I got the point, and the irresponsibility changed. That's a nice example of how to discipline creatively. Giving a child extra work, making him clean up a mess or fix what was broken (or at least *try* to) can help that child to learn a more important lesson than he would learn from a spanking.

It doesn't matter if the child seems to enjoy a consequence that you give him for misbehavior. Even if he hates sitting in a chair, he is going to pretend it's a game in order to convince you that it doesn't work. Then you will resort to the punishment he's looking for—a spanking! If you put a child in his room and he does not stay there, simply continue taking him back to his room each time he comes out, saying, "The timeout will begin as soon as you stay in your room." Eventually, after many repetitions, he will learn that you mean business, and he will stay in his room.

The general guideline for timeouts is one minute for every

year of the child's age. But I have some guidelines that I like better because they require the child to take responsibility for what he did. I suggest saying, "You will stay in timeout until you can tell me three things:

1. what you did that was wrong
2. what you should have done instead
3. how you will do right the next time."

But this is not the only form of discipline available. Grounding a child, limiting television, making him go to bed a little early, giving him extra chores, are all ways to teach a child that certain behaviors simply will not be tolerated.

Don't worry about the consequences not being serious enough. If a child breaks something and has to clean it up, you might not feel it is punishment enough, especially if the object was expensive or full of memories. But you have allowed your child to amend for his error by cleaning up after himself. And when you do this consistently, he will begin to be more careful.

WHEN GRANDMA BABY-SITS

Because my husband and I both work, we leave our small children with their grandmother during the day. But we're discovering the hard way that Grandmother has different ideas about discipline than we do. Often when we correct our children about something, they'll say, "Well, Grandmother lets us do this." Do you have any suggestions?

Grandmothers who baby-sit have to play a dual role. They essentially wear two hats. They are *grandma* and they are *baby-sitter*. So you, as parents, need to try to understand that.

Since children are born manipulators, it doesn't take them

long to discover that one way of making you give in to them is to quote their grandmother. So you may want to take what they say with a little bit of doubt.

Here are some ideas for solving these problems. First, have a loving but clear and straightforward talk with Grandmother. Make your values and the goals that you have set for your children clear to her. Seek her help and cooperation in achieving these. Help her to understand that while she would like to be Grandmother, she is playing the role of baby-sitter, and you need help in enforcing the rules and exerting the discipline your children need. Still, because she *is* a grandmother, the results may not be all that you desire. You may have to work at this from the other side of the problem also. That is, make it clear to your children that grandmas are special people who have the right to spoil them a little bit, *but* rules are different at home. Parents do not want to spoil their children. Also, children should not take advantage of Grandmother's love and indulgence.

I think you need to be very careful that you not develop a spirit of resentment toward this grandmother. Be careful that you do not give in to jealous feelings towards her. You will always be the parent of your children. You can earn their respect, you can gain their love, and you can also enjoy (so they can enjoy) the services of their grandmother as a baby-sitter.

GREEDINESS

How can I keep my daughter from asking our friends and relatives to give her gifts on her birthday and at other special times? I'm embarrassed by it, and I feel it's improper to ask.

In general, teaching proper behavior requires only a few simple steps. Following through with those steps is the hard part. I recommend that parents make a very simple, clear, and definite rule. That rule goes something like this: *Don't do* ____. Instead of saying, "I wish you wouldn't ask" or "You really shouldn't ask Grandmother for a gift," be very clear and say *emphatically,* "Don't ask for gifts." The child will understand exactly what you mean when you make it that clear. Keep the basic relationship between you and the child loving and positive. Such a relationship is the motivator for the child's cooperation with whatever rules you establish.

Have a consequence available if your child does break the rule. Take the gift away until she has written a thank-you note, for example, or until some other condition has been met.

EXPANDING LIMITS

What advice do you have for parents who are concerned about future teenage rebellion?

The advice that I have is related to a story I heard very recently. That was of a twenty-two-year-old man who was working full-time with a very fine job and good income. He still lived at home with his parents, and they required that he be at home by 10:30, no matter where he went. He was not allowed to get his own apartment until he was married, and he was not prepared for marriage just yet. Here was a man who had a seriously overprotective family that did not allow him the normal sort of freedom of a man of twenty-two (and a godly young man at that!).

The wise parent observes each child's readiness for a new level of growth and responsibility—and beats the child to the draw, so to speak. When parents give a child additional freedoms, *before* the child asks for them and because he has earned them by taking responsibility, the child will rarely need to rebel. Your awareness of your child's readiness to grow and expand his horizons will prevent a great deal of unnecessary teenage rebellion.

TEACHING SELF-CONTROL

Sometimes self-control means going against what comes most naturally to a child. I'm wondering if it's even possible to teach a boy or girl that kind of self-discipline.

The steps in teaching self-control are not very difficult. It's remembering to teach them that is hard for parents. You need to have your goal very clear, and that goal is to *teach your child to overcome that instinctive desire to explode with the emotion of the moment.*

Once the goal is established, you need to plan a route to get to the goal. You need to guide the child through the process several times, if you expect her to learn to control her feelings and express them appropriately. Let me emphasize that you ought not to teach your child to hide those feelings. She needs to express the anger, rage, or fear, *but* she can learn to do that in a controlled fashion rather than a destructive one. The process involves three steps:

1. Verbalize the feeling.
2. Explain why you feel as you do.
3. Determine what you will do about the problem.

Teach your child the vocabulary with which to express her feelings. Once you have walked and talked your child through this process several times, allow her to try it alone, and see how successful she is. Cheer her successes royally and remind her gently when she forgets.

Parents must model this behavior. It's one thing to teach

your children to exercise control, but you must also avoid blowing your top. Your example will be the most effective teaching tool of all.

STRONG-WILLED CHILD

I have a six-year-old son who is extremely strong-willed. He can be loving and giving, but he continually challenges our authority and is determined to do as he pleases. We would appreciate any suggestions you might have that would help us. How should we discipline him?

This parent needs to be aware that every strong-willed child has at least one strong-willed parent, which inevitably causes power struggles. In power struggles we too often lose sight of *what* is right in a situation, in the interest of proving *who* is right.

What do you do, then, in teaching a willful child?

Develop a plan. Sit down together (yes, even with the child) and make a brief list of your expectations for behavior. Decide what will happen when he does his very best (is there a reward?) and what will happen when he doesn't (is there a negative consequence?). In my opinion natural consequences—letting the child face the results of his actions—are best in most cases (much more effective than spanking).

Take one issue at a time and work on gaining compliance with it, then go on to the next area of conflict. Choose the time wisely when you are going to work on an issue. Give yourselves plenty of time and energy, such as during a weekend or the summertime, when the child's schedule and yours may be a little easier. Avoid arguing, and stick with your plan.

Levy consequences such as the loss of a privilege like

television time or playtime. Whatever is important to your child can motivate him to work with you on correcting the problems. Be persistent. Do not give in. Whether the child acts indifferent, angry, or sad, be firm and consistent. When he learns that you're in control, your child will give in and the next issue will be easier. Give him as much positive feedback as you can, and remind him how much you love him.

EXPLAIN REQUESTS?

We have a three-year-old son. When his mother or I tell him he can't do something, how much should we reason with him or explain? Is it all right to make him behave in a certain way, just because we say so, or is this a cop-out?

I think what this father is really asking is, how much authority should he use in dealing with his child? Authority is a very important concept to understand. It seems to me that it is ultimately possible only if it is reasonable, fair, and in the best interests of everyone involved. Authority is certainly based on the strength and wisdom of the parents. But if that wisdom is not conveyed through explanation, I think the child is likely to resent the discipline.

Good discipline, then, teaches right *principles* for living. These basic policies are applied in many little events. In our family, for example, we had a rule that we do not hurt each other physically or verbally—so we didn't need a number of rules that said, "Don't hit, don't pull hair, don't kick, don't pinch."

Once these rules are established and explained, then little further explanation is needed. Don't argue your case with a child. One simple explanation is enough. After that, a firm, "Do it!" will establish positive authority.

TEACHING CAUTION

What are some of the cautions that you think every child should be taught?

There are a number, but I'd like to remind you that children fortunately are born with a *sense* of caution. Children are born with a fear of loud noises and a fear of falling, so that inborn, God-given fear is the element that parents can build on in teaching good judgment and healthy cautiousness in all of life.

Going chronologically through a child's life, the first caution that should be taught is that a child must be warned of *physical dangers.* Toddlers need to be taught to stay out of the street, away from cars, off of high places, away from hot objects, and away from water if no adult is around. They can learn that car seats are the only place they sit in cars. As they get older and the locks come off the cupboards, preschoolers can learn that some household supplies are poisonous. They also learn how to fasten their own seat belts and to use seatbelts every time they ride. School-age children need to be taught bicycle and skate safety (especially the proper use of helmets), water safety (even in the bath), and safety when home alone. You can probably think of many more areas of safety. All can be taught, though the age of the child must be considered.

I would strongly recommend that you teach children to observe safety precautions *whether or not you are there.*

A second area of caution is how to handle *natural disasters or threats.* In my part of the country, we have tornadoes and thunderstorms. Lightning can strike and kill people, so children must be taught where to seek shelter if they are caught in a thunderstorm. In other parts of the country, earthquakes, avalanches, and hurricanes are natural disasters that can strike an area. Children must learn where to go to find safety.

In homes, there is another area of safety that must be taught, and that is *fire protection.* Recently I met with a family whose home had been destroyed by fire. Because they knew how to get out of the house safely, no one was hurt.

Sadly, in today's world we must also teach our children to avoid strangers, bullies at school, or even neighbors and relatives who try to touch them inappropriately. *Teach your child to judge wisely,* to behave cautiously, and to talk things over with you, and you may well prevent some needless tragedies in their lives.

CONSEQUENCES

What discipline and consequences would you suggest for lying and bad language?

First, discover why your child is lying or swearing. The most common reasons are to gain attention from peers, get out of certain duties, or make themselves feel important.

The child who lies or swears is nearly always insecure and lacks a healthy self-confidence. As you step back and evaluate your parenting, you may discover that you have been too harsh, perhaps a bit inconsistent (letting lies work now and then), and that you have not balanced your punishments with enough love and congeniality.

Start the discipline, then, by changing your patterns according to the need. Be firm and consistent, but keep a caring and kindly attitude. Your child will learn even more effectively from kindness if you follow through.

Do make it clear that lying will not be tolerated and that there will be consequences. For example, if your child tells you she has cleaned her room when she really hasn't, go with her to clean it at once and allow her to miss playtime or delay her dinner until it is done.

For swearing, I suggest a child pay a fine for each unacceptable word. This fine may be taken out of his allowance, or he may be assigned a job to earn the money owed.

Be sure to explain clearly why these habits are harmful and that it is out of love that you are punishing him. If you really mean that, your child will recognize your concern and, sooner or later, he will comply.

REWARDS

I would like to know how you can motivate children to work on their own at home and in school without always having to reward them. Our daughter is very bright, but she would rather talk or watch others work, instead of going ahead and getting her own work done.

This is a common problem. I recommend that parents talk through this issue. When you have determined a plan that sounds practical, then discuss it with your child. Let that child know there is going to be a new routine: the question is not going to be *whether* she will do the assigned job but *when,* and let her know that every pleasure stops until her responsibility is taken care of. Start with a household task that is reasonably time-limited, one that perhaps the entire family could work on together. At least one parent needs to work with the child in order to teach her how to organize her work and actually finish it. My experience has shown that children who are given responsibilities at home with consistent follow through will also be responsible at school.

The best reward for any child is your pride and pleasure in her achievements, and eventually her own self-respect. It takes effort and time from you as parents to make that happen, but that time is perhaps one of the best investments that you can make in your child's future.

FORGETFULNESS

Other than constant nagging, what can parents do to help children remember things?

In order to avoid nagging, simply rely on natural consequences. That is, if the child is late to meals, the family goes right ahead and eats, and whatever part of the meal that child misses, he misses, until the next meal comes along. You do not rewarm the food, you do not extend the mealtime, you do not rescue the child. Likewise, if the child forget to take his lunch to school, he goes hungry or begs or borrows money in order to get lunch. That's one lunchtime that he will remember—perhaps the next day when he is starting out the door again without a lunch.

Be sure you praise your child's good qualities and reflect on those so that he does not feel like a failure. If your child is forgetting because he is thinking about something worrisome, try to find out what it is and deal with it.

Finally, some kids just have more trouble than others remembering details. Often these children have ADD or another learning disability and cannot help themselves. They need understanding and strategies for success. Here are a few ideas:

- Write a list—on a piece of paper, on a calendar, on a dry-erase board on the bedroom door or on the refrigerator.

- Use a watch with an alarm to remind the child of appointments.

- Write up checklists to enumerate all the steps in a process (e.g. a checklist of things one must do and items one must pack before leaving for school).

- Avoid nagging so your child will not learn to get by on your sense of responsibility. Let natural consequences teach him.

ALLOWANCES

Do you think children should receive a certain amount of money each week to spend as they wish?

Yes, if that is possible. There are some wonderful lessons that can be taught to young children by giving them an allowance. Money should be given to children to help them understand how money is to be used and what its value actually is.

Teaching children to budget is possible by the age of six or eight. If you can afford to give your child even a dollar, give it to him in change, so that he can save a dime, give a dime to Sunday school, and spend a couple of dimes on whatever he might be able to buy. Help the child to know he will have no other money to spend that week for frivolous or unnecessary items.

Be consistent. Increase the child's allowance as his responsibility increases, and you will have taught him a valuable financial lesson.

PAY FOR HOUSEHOLD CHORES?

My young teenage daughter always wants to earn money for chores she does in the house. She's forever asking me if there is something she can do, and how much I will pay her for doing it. I'm going broke. Help!

Some children feel that they must be paid for every household job they do. I can understand children wanting money, but the fact is that many parents fall into a trap of paying for everything! My philosophy is that everyone within the family should help with chores. Everyone needs to learn to give as well as to get, and the family is the arena for learning that.

There *is* a positive side to what this daughter is saying, however. She is not asking for a donation. She is at least willing to earn money. So while this mother is upset, I hope she will look at that good point in this issue.

I suggest she hold a family council meeting to decide on a budget for each family member. Household tasks must be done by each family member without pay. Those basic jobs should be assigned and rotated fairly among all of the family members. (A family council is a wonderful place in which to decide on these.)

Over and above these basic jobs, however, there may be some special jobs that are up for bid for extra pay. Whatever pay those jobs merit can be settled together and then written down. Encourage your children, as soon as they are able to seek jobs outside of the home, to find out about those possibilities, as well as jobs within the house. Lawn care for neighbors, child care, helping someone else clean house—all of those are time-honored jobs that children, too young to get jobs in a commercial establishment, can do to earn money. Then teach money management to your children. They need to know that there are limits as to how much money is available and that they must budget the way they spend it.

CHEATING

It was very upsetting and embarrassing when my child's teacher called and said he had been caught cheating. Why is it that some children just give in to the urge to cheat, even though their parents have stressed honesty and playing by the rules?

Frankly, the motivation for most cheating is understandable and positive. Children cheat because they want to do well, and every parent and teacher wants the children to do well, too. The problem is that they have somehow learned how to do well without putting in the honest effort that it takes to learn the material. Interestingly, most cheating begins quite by accident. One child sees another do it and get away with it. The opportunity then presents itself to him, and in a moment of weakness, he gives in and finds that he has done quite well because he cheated.

The payoff has seemed to teach the child that cheating pays. Grades get better. You can get by (the child reasons) without putting in so much work, and so why not do it? Our society, in fact, teaches us to look for easy ways. I suspect there is a bit of natural laziness in all of us that really prefers to take the easy way toward success.

The important thing, once parents understand something of why the child cheats, is understanding what to do about it. Having worked in schools for some twenty years, I am appalled at the number of parents who take exception to the reports of misbehavior. Often I find parents taking the child's side, even when the child is clearly doing something wrong. Your first step needs to be to team up with the school or the person who has become aware of the cheating.

Watch your own child carefully. See if he wins by cheating when he plays games with brothers and sisters. See if there are other little evidences of dishonesty that begin to grow. When you see these, do not ask the child if he is doing them or why he is doing them, because he will promptly deny them. But do reveal to your child what you have seen. Explain to him that these things are dishonest; they will not be tolerated; and then set about changing his behavior according to these steps:

First, *check your own lives.* Your children will be quick to pick up your example, so if you have not been completely honest, work hard to shape up your own lives. Second, *explain* to your child directly that you will not tolerate cheating and dishonesty. *Set up a consequence* for any time the child breaks a rule, whether at home or at school, and follow through with those consequences. Finally, *praise* your child for changing that habit. *Correct* him when he does not, and you will win this very important issue.

BLACKMAIL

How should parents answer when their children try emotional blackmail?

In my experience, a child blackmailing a parent is symptomatic of the child's having accumulated too much power in that family. It is the *parents* who should have the power. I think many families today have reversed the old parental role in which my father, for example, would say, "If you don't do this, Grace, then this will happen," and I knew it would. Today I'm hearing children say to their parents, "Mom, if you don't let me do this, then I will run away," or whatever. That's a very frightening situation for the child as well as the parents.

Let me give you examples of *what not to do:*

- do not act worried or upset, because that may imply that you believe the child has the power to do what he is threatening.

- do not counteract that child's threats with pleading. Be strong; act as an adult and do not try to get the child's love or happiness back too quickly. Dealing with the situation is far more important than keeping your child happy all the time.

When you face an emotional blackmail: First, *clarify what the issue is.* Why is the child threatening and upset? What is the problem? When you find this out, talk about it. For a younger child, you may need to put into words the child's feelings, because often a child does not have the vocabulary to express that. "I know you are angry or scared [or whatever], and here's what I think you need . . ." As a parent, when you verbalize what the child is going through, you will help him to calm down and thus alleviate the stress that's making him attempt this blackmail job.

Second, *decide what you can do together* about the problem.

TATTLING

At what point does tattling become a serious problem?

There *can* be a fine line between tattling and reporting a dangerous or alarming situation that needs adult attention. The difference that helps me understand which is actually happening is whether or not the reporting is intended to get the other child *in trouble* or to keep the other child *from harm.* That's a very important concept for parents and teachers alike to understand.

Usually a child tattles because that child has no other means of gaining favor from the adult, so she tattles in order to get adult attention (and also to make herself look better than those "bad" children). This, of course, is a child who is not very secure and who has to resort to this means of seeking self-esteem. The tattler is almost always insecure; she has had her feelings hurt; she may be angry; and she feels inadequate. She needs regular feedback that focuses on her good points, building up her self-esteem.

Well, what can you do if you have a tattling child? I recommend that you *explain what is wrong* with the habit itself and *insist that the child stop it.* Set up a reminding system for yourselves as parents to follow through in stopping that particular habit. Then search for the source that may have caused the anger and the insecurity. Work very hard to correct the problems that have produced that situation. Promoting a sense of maturity and an honest sense of responsibility in your child can replace that bad habit with a very good one by using the child's concern and compassion for others.

10

SPIRITUAL TRAINING

TEACHING AN INFANT ABOUT GOD

What can a mother do in the first years of life to teach a child about God? Is prayer all we do at this age?

Prayer is an essential element in our child's upbringing. But it is not all we can do to introduce that child to God. The most vital part of a baby's life is the development of trust. That sense of trust in Mother and Father is the quality that is later transferred to trusting the heavenly Father. As the new parents comfort their little baby, provide for his safety, cuddle him with strength and warmth, provide joy and stimulation, and feed the baby, they are teaching that child the basic sense of trust that is so important to developing faith. God designed parents to teach a little child what God is like.

As the child grows, you can sing to him about Jesus' love, read stories about God's care and forgiveness, model God's care and forgiveness for him, and then give him books to read about God.

EXPLAINING GOD TO SMALL CHILDREN

What words would you use to explain God to a small child?

That's a difficult question, because a great many adults do not have a good concept of God. When I give psychiatric evaluations to people, one of the questions I routinely ask them is what they think about God and what God looks like. I receive a variety of answers. To many adults he is a harsh, punishing parent. To some he is a wise, loving impersonal power. How God enters into your lives as parents determines how you will communicate him to your child.

One of my best learning experiences in understanding God was the time that my father had me watch a baby chick pecking its way out of its shell. He taught me that God is a wise Creator who had a wonderful plan for how things should happen in nature. My brother explained to me how lightning releases nitrates into the soil, and yet lightning and thunder had been very frightening to me. Understanding that they had a purpose made God's power magnificent to me. The cycle of water from the lake to vapor in the air to rain that waters the soil was another example, as I studied science, of God's marvelous handiwork. Walking through fields of wheat or a garden made me aware of the teamwork that humans and God have together.

When you speak to a child about God, try to include these concepts:

- God is *loving and warm.* When I taught my children this and read them stories from the Bible, I would hold them on my lap and demonstrate to them, physically, the love and warmth of human parenting. I taught them to compare that with God's heavenly parenting.

- God is *wise.* He knows all things, past, present, and future.

- God is *powerful.* He can defeat any enemy.

- God is *creative.* He called all the worlds into being.

- God *forgives.* There is nothing we can do that can separate us from the love of God. You can help your children to understand this by forgiving them when they have done something wrong.

All these essential characteristics make up a healthy view of God. Children learn these through learning from parents, reading their Bibles (there are many beautiful, simple new versions), and worshiping with other children who believe.

TEACHING YOUR CHILD TO PRAY

What special lifelong lessons about prayer can be taught only in the context of everyday family living?

If your child attends Sunday school regularly, then no doubt he or she is learning certain Bible stories there. But I hope you haven't left all of your children's spiritual training to the church experts, especially in the area of praying, because no one is in the position that you are to demonstrate to your child how prayer enters into everyday life.

I think almost all of my lessons about prayer came from my family. I recently had an experience with my oldest daughter and my grandson that I'd like to share with you, because it's such a wonderful example of the practicality of prayer in a child's life. She and her son, our grandson, had watched a television program in which a mother was suffering from cancer and had to make decisions about giving away her children. Andy was horrified by the program. (They had not anticipated that it would be so sad, and that perhaps he should not have watched it.) He had bad dreams for a number of nights after watching that movie; his mother realized that the movie was a part of those bad dreams.

They were talking about God one day, when Andy said to his mother, "Mommy, maybe if we ask God, he'll take away my bad dreams." So that night at bedtime they prayed for that mother with cancer, and they prayed about those bad dreams. God answered that prayer for sleep, and Andy slept very peacefully from that night on. It was a wonderful lesson in faith for him, as well as for his mother, and a renewal of my own faith came out of that special story.

CULTS

Is there a certain type of person who is more vulnerable to the lure of cult groups?

Yes, there is such a person, but perhaps it would be helpful to start with a description of the characteristics of a cult. There are so many new groups springing up around our country today that it is sometimes hard for parents and young people to know whether a group really is basically Christian or a cult. Several of the cultic characteristics that are easily detected are these:

1. *Rigid structure* and unbending rules, usually with one *very strong authority figure.* There is always a charismatic leader, someone who is easy to follow and who is very dynamic. Almost always in today's current cults, this is a man.

2. *Indoctrination or brainwashing* that includes sleep deprivation, lack of privacy, intensive structuring of the entire day, restricted contact with family and former friends, and other mind-control techniques.

3. *Severing of family ties.* Cults (and gangs also, by the way)

aim to keep followers both physically and emotionally distant from families. The cult group wants to replace the role previously played by family and friends.

There are several types of people who are susceptible to the cults. First are those who are adventurous, exploring types—young people who have their minds open to anything and everything. They may have little discernment or experience and little training in how to make value judgments. These young people, however, while susceptible to cults, oftentimes are also wise enough and strong-willed enough to get out of them.

The second group of people worry me more. This is the type of young person who is lonely and who lacks a close relationship with a parent (often the father). Through the cult such people may seek friends, a sense of belonging, and a father figure. The cult offers such people the family togetherness that they crave.

Another group of young people who are susceptible to cults are those who have low self-esteem, high dependency needs, and a willingness to submit to authority, even if it is bad. People who are compliant and easy to get along with adapt well to cults.

Every parent and young person needs to be able to recognize the characteristics and structure of exploitive cults today so they are prepared to avoid them.

FAMILY PRAYER TIME

How can we make family prayer time more exciting for our teenager? to make this a real family time?

That question reminds me of my growing-up years when prayer time was a beautiful part of our family's schedule for the day. I would like to recommend a classic book written by Rosalind Rinker. It's called *Prayer: Conversing with God.*

Rinker was the first person who taught me that prayer is simply talking with God. Doing this as a family brings the presence of God into the heart of the family. This can be a natural and warm part of every family's day.

For teenagers, prayer must be centered in reality. I don't believe they really go much for long prayers or idealistic kinds of prayers. Teenagers are looking for their own identities, and their independence is of great concern to them (and you). They explore, they disagree, they challenge and doubt. All of those characteristics are essential in learning to pray. How they see God, of course, must involve seeing him as real, understanding, powerful enough to be doubted and challenged, and loving enough to come back to a warm relationship when they have moved past their doubts and rebelliousness. Bible readings together need to show the actions and feelings of God. The Gospel of Mark is an action book, and one that bring us the very living dynamic of Jesus Christ: Christ in the temple, stilling the storm, energetic, honest, compassionate, and wise. These are all qualities that I think would appeal to any teenager.

In prayers, I recommend that there be some *praise,* because we all need to worship and adore the heavenly Father. But I would recommend for teenagers that there be more expression of *gratitude* for God's past help in their lives and for the answers to the prayers they have prayed. Specific *requests* for today's needs are a normal, natural expression of a teenager's prayers. As you pray for Sally's test and John's date tonight, I think it will help them to know that God is really concerned in the little affairs of their lives, as well as the big ones. Moms and dads, don't forget to pray for patience and wisdom for yourselves. Real conversational prayer is just that.

SUNDAY-SCHOOL DROPOUT

What can you do if your child doesn't want to go to

Sunday school? My eleven-year-old son says that it's boring. His class seems to be fine and the teacher is good, so I'm baffled about my son's resistance. Will I be helping him any if I insist on his attending?

The reasons children should attend Sunday school are fairly obvious. We want them to learn about God, his Word, and his world. We want them to see the importance of the church and its function in their lives and the world in general. And we want our children to make friends with those who share our spiritual values.

There are also several reasons why children resist going to Sunday school. Some, unfortunately, resist going because they want to reject their parents' values or win a power struggle. Also, children are often influenced by their peers to think that Sunday school is kid stuff for "wimps." And Sunday school is, sometimes, juvenile or irrelevant if it is not geared to the specific age or needs of children. Sometimes children have stayed up too late the night before and are too tired to get up for Sunday school.

Today's children are spoiled by having so much entertainment available to them. They come to believe that everything should be entertaining and exciting, and Sunday school just can't always be that.

Whatever the reason, parents should be clear about the value of Sunday school and explain those reasons to your child in a logical and firm fashion. Also be clear about your expectations for attendance. Your child does not have a choice about attending regular school, and I think he does not need to have a choice about attending Sunday school and most youth activities, even through high school. If you disagree, then make it clear to your son at what age he can begin to choose whether to go.

However, sometimes refusing Sunday school is just a way a rebellious child can get back at you. Have you caused some hurt in his life that has resulted in resentment and a need to get even? Or are you in a power struggle? If so, try to heal those interpersonal issues and see if the Sunday-school issue disappears.

Also, constructively take a look at your son's class. See if it is the kind of environment that would attract him and make him want to go and gain some profitable experiences there. Help your church make your Sunday school truly worthwhile. There is a great variety of Sunday school curricula, and one of them ought to be right for your son's class. You always help your child when you teach spiritual values, self-discipline, obedience, and respect.

BIG PEOPLE'S CHURCH

We want our preschooler to begin joining us in church on Sunday nights, since she is too old for the nursery and no junior church is available. So far every attempt has been embarrassing, with lots of whispering, crawling, and distractions. Other kids her age are joining their parents. Should we persevere and hope for the best, or wait a while and try again later?

I can still vividly recall feeling bored and as if I absolutely could not sit still for one more minute in church! Fortunately, my parents were quite understanding. My mother had a way with a pencil and paper, and when she realized that I simply could not tolerate one more minute, she would take out that paper and with her pencil create the most marvelous pictures. Then my father would have his turn. In his suit pocket he kept a sack of wintergreen candies. When he knew that I simply could not sit still another minute, he would rustle that paper very softly, and I knew that help was on the way. That paper and piece of candy got me through those endless moments.

Church really is not geared to preschoolers, and perhaps cannot be. What they can learn from adult church is quite limited. I think it's ideal if a children's church or activity time is available. If this is not an option, however, the parents need to train the child to sit still.

If it's necessary for your preschooler to be in church, try going in for a short period of time, then take her outside for a time, and then back in, so that she gradually becomes accustomed to the time and the structure of the service. Gradually increase the child's time to sit still. Use some firmness in requiring a little extra time and attention each week, so the child will increasingly be able to tolerate sitting still.

Also, provide some quiet distractions, such as plastic water-filled games, activity books, handicrafts like friendship bracelets and, for older kids, good Christian books. Above all, be careful to keep God's house a place to which you and your child love to go.

11

SOCIAL DEVELOPMENT

GOOD JUDGMENT

How can I teach my child to be discerning, without being too picky or expecting perfection? I'm afraid he may become too rigid—a difficult person to please.

That's an interesting question and one that brings up a very important value in my life. *Discernment* means an ability to evaluate and choose what is best for the people involved. I think discernment is a great gift to have. And, it is a quality that can be taught.

Here are some suggestions as to how parents might teach discernment to their children: First, I believe *parents must start with themselves* and their example. Look through your own decision-making methods. How do you decide what is good nutrition for yourself and your family? How do you balance your food intake, the times for your meals, mealtime topics of conversation, the mood, the sense of intimacy that focuses around mealtimes? Discernment can be played out and exemplified in such practical areas. Your choice of friends, your lifestyle decisions, your home atmosphere, your priorities, your work ethic—all of those topics demand good judgment or discernment.

Here are some simple, practical suggestions for teaching a young child to make good choices:

Give your child limited choices within the framework of his ability to choose, such as having a whole glass or a half glass of juice for breakfast; whether he wants to wear a green sweatshirt or a blue one with jeans. Compliment your child on those choices that show good taste.

Give the child feedback when he makes choices that are not quite so good. Help him to see how to choose more wisely the next time, without being too critical or condemning. For example, if he made fun of a friend on the playground, help him to see how that friend might have been hurt by that. Help him to see other ways of solving the same problem.

Tell someone else in the child's hearing about his growing sense of good judgment. These small, daily choices will eventually be translated into good judgment in the more complex, moral areas of life. Good emotional health is evidenced by the decisions we make. Discernment makes such decisions possible, for you and your child.

DEVELOPING INDEPENDENCE

My kids seem to be going through a stage when they are challenging everything their mother and I say. We want to encourage them to be independent, yet we're also concerned about keeping them safe. How can we deal with this power struggle without feeling inadequate or doubting ourselves?

Two of the characteristics of adolescents are that they are confused in their thinking and ambivalent or mixed-up in their feelings. Being able to discuss, argue, and debate without becoming angry or rejecting can help children to think through those confused ideas and come to really solid values and beliefs. Children also need parents who are willing to make a case for their time-tested values, and yet brave enough to let those young people try out some ideas for themselves. You do have to draw some lines on that, and you have to be wise and strong enough to hold those lines firmly in order to protect those children.

Children need parents who are loving enough to be tough, and yet can still be tender. Young people need parents who are congenial enough to enjoy them and secure enough to admit their own mistakes (and even to laugh at themselves, but *never* to laugh at the children). Congeniality and a sense of humor can tide almost any family over those rough times. Young people need parents who are patient enough to wait out this fatiguing and often frightening time in life.

RAISING A GOOD FUTURE SPOUSE

What can parents teach their children now about being a good husband or wife later?

The characteristics of a good adult, be it husband, wife, or single, start with these qualities:

1. *The ability to give and receive with generosity and gratitude.* Far too often, I find people unable to give, and on the other hand, unable to ask or receive from anyone else. This ability must include giving physical affection as well as material things.

2. *The ability to be open, honest, and trusting.* Real intimacy that is involved in a good relationship within families or within friendships depends upon these qualities. Obviously being open and trusting must be balanced with the development of

good judgment. There need to be some areas of privacy, and we don't have to be open to the extent of telling everything we know to everyone.

3. *The ability to handle loss or disappointment* and to grieve with simplicity and sincerity is essential to being a good parent, a good friend, or a good spouse.

4. *The ability to respect oneself and the other person,* to be proud of one another, and to build up one another—to express the pride that we feel *with* one another *to* one another.

5. *The ability to negotiate,* to work through disagreements with respect and love for one another.

6. *The ability to delay gratification.* Being able to hold off on some immediate pleasure in order to gain some higher good later on.

How do you teach these to your little child? First and most importantly, by modeling. By demonstrating these qualities toward one another as mother and father. Second, I think you teach these to your children by sitting down with them now and then and verbally giving them guidelines for how they must get along with one another, as well as with you. Third, through the methods of discipline and training that you employ, you teach your little child to begin developing the qualities that will help him grow up to be a wonderful friend, a good spouse, and a marvelous parent.

SELF-ESTEEM OR HAUGHTINESS?

How can I increase my child's self-confidence without creating the kind of pride the Bible teaches against?

Egotistical pride is obnoxious to everyone. But true self-confidence is the very best protection against false or "carnal" pride. Ironically, pride and conceit are often the result of low self-esteem and represent a person's intense effort to prove that he or she really *is* somebody important, when in actual fact, that person does not feel important at all.

Healthy self-esteem includes having good, biblical values based on a knowledge that we are children of the heavenly Father. When we think about being children of the Father (children of the King!), that is something that should indicate the respect and honor that God has for us. Furthermore, whatever assets, talents, or abilities we have truly are gifts from God. Whatever is good in me becomes a responsibility—pleasurable and rewarding to be sure, but nevertheless a responsibility. Pride, on the other hand, really does not acknowledge God or the benefits that others give us in developing those gifts. Pride says, "Look at me! See what *I* did?"

Teach your child that her special gifts come from God and are for appreciating and sharing, and haughtiness will not be a part of her character.

AN UNGRATEFUL CHILD

What can parents do to help a child who has established a pattern of being ungrateful?

Some parents have difficulty saying no to their kids. The United States is a culture of affluence. After the Depression of the 1930s and the war of the 1940s, an entire generation of parents wanted their children to have everything they had not been able to enjoy. Meanwhile, science continued to produce new and exciting inventions for pleasure. Motorized toys, talking dolls, video and computer games are all for children's pleasure. Advertising has made all of these things very obvious to children, and the presentation of exciting new items is a daily occurrence on television.

If parents want to break the habit of materialism, here's a

system that's certain to cure the problem if parents have the courage to follow it: First, *begin by being aware that you have given much to your children.* Second, *find ways of showing emotional warmth without gifts.* Telling happy jokes, playing a game together, planning an outing that would really be fun—not costly and not sophisticated—can help your children to know that simple happenings can satisfy their cravings. Third, *stop giving gifts,* except small, carefully selected ones for very special events. When the child asks for more, explain your new philosophy of giving less and enjoying more what you have.

If your child wants a special item, require him to work and save for it. Give him extra jobs, perhaps, and help him earn money himself. You will find he will be much more appreciative when he has had to sweat to earn it. Require your child to express gratitude and do that yourself. As you teach and model for your child the spirit of gratitude, I think you will find your own joy in life increasing, as well as your pride in your child.

INFLUENCES

Who has the greatest influence on a child?

That answer depends upon the family. When parents are really involved in the lives of their children, then *they* are the greatest influence. A recent study has verified that even for rebellious teens, their parents have the greatest influence. Parents must remember this and keep the influence loving, wise, and strong.

But when parents become too busy or involved with other concerns and neglect their children, then other influences come into play. Many people today are concerned about the impact of a child's *friends,* as well as the influence of *teachers* who may not always be very godly people. These are concerns I share. *Television* has an impact on most of us because it is on in our homes so much of the time. If we are not careful and alert, so that we can counteract the messages of the commercials and the programs, then television can powerfully affect our children.

Mothers and fathers can be the most powerful influence in the lives of their children. In the preadolescent period, *mother is generally the major force.* The father is present, and his influence varies with his involvement with the family. Mother's best influence comes in a unique balance: that of nurturing and guiding—a positive criticalness to discern the problems and dangers in a child's life. Through her womanhood she can help her son understand how to relate to the opposite sex, and she can model femininity and self-respect for her daughter.

Fathers become more influential in the teenage years, though we now know that they are very important in the preschool days. The father demonstrates the protection, guidance, and teaching that a male can offer if he is willing to assume that responsibility. His approval and disapproval are very powerful factors in a young person's life. He, too, offers a role model for his son to become a man and for his daughter to relate to the opposite sex.

SELF-ESTEEM

What can parents do to help a boy or girl who feels insecure?

You can help a child with poor self-esteem in many ways:

Love unconditionally. Children must be loved for who they are and not for what they do. That acceptance and love should be communicated with absolute honesty. You cannot pretend to love a child and have him believe it. It must be real.

Discipline firmly, lovingly, and consistently. Your child will learn to be and do the things that are worthy of pride and self-respect.

Express pride. Tell your child you like what he does and who he is. Be careful to avoid a mixture of approval and disapproval. Never say to a child, "That's fine but . . ." In my experience the *but* always eliminates the *fine* in the mind of a child. The best compliments are specific rather than generic. A child will more easily hear and accept, "I love the colors you chose to wear today. You really have an eye for how things go together" rather than "That's a great outfit."

Be positive. Laugh and play together. When life becomes heavy and is a worry, children lose a very important ingredient in the building of self-esteem. So work at keeping an attitude and atmosphere of congeniality, warmth, and laughter, which, as the Bible so beautifully says, "does good like a medicine."

Listen to your child. Spend time with your child so that he feels valued. Talk to him about feelings and try to find out if he frequently criticizes himself or berates himself. If he does, try to teach him how to accept his mistakes and forgive himself. If he does not, find out if someone else criticizes him a lot—a parent, grandparent, or neighbor, for instance.

Talk to your child. Share your thoughts, feelings, interests, and desires with your child. This models good communication for them and helps them feel that you value them enough to talk to them about personal things.

Help him shine at something. Work at exploring new interests, abilities, and activities. Look for a skill your child can develop further. Then spend time with him and help him develop it. As your child grows in skills that he can share with playmates, you will find that the friendliness automatically happens. Children will crowd around him to learn the exciting new skill that he has mastered.

Encourage making friends. Help your child with his social

adjustments. When you or he finds some new friends, maybe one or two at a time, let him bring them into your home, where you can observe your child and encourage him to play comfortably and successfully.

Solicit your child's help. Asking him for a back rub or a bit of advice on a perplexing problem will make your child feel that he is making a real contribution and being a big help.

Seek outside advice. Finally, do not hesitate to seek a counselor to help your child if you believe that he has a serious problem with self-esteem. Sometimes an impartial friend can help a child to feel more confident and valued.

ENEMIES OF SELF-ESTEEM

What are some of the enemies of self-esteem that parents need to guard against?

One of the most important enemies is that of the *parents' negative attitude.* I find a great many parents approach their responsibilities as mother and father by feeling that it's their main job to discover what is wrong with their children and correct it. So be sure that your attitude as parents is positive, and that you look for the strengths more than for the defects.

Another enemy is *chronic marital strife.* A child can hardly feel secure and confident when she daily fears losing one of her parents. When you argue intensely and regularly, children are afraid that one of you may leave.

Discrediting each other as mother and father, finding fault, or criticizing each other in front of the child can also make her feel inadequate. Whether you like it or not, the child will see herself as being like one or the other of you, and criticizing each other indirectly condemns the child. This is a particular problem for divorcing parents, as the ex-spouse often comes in for a lot of criticism in front of the children. Remember that when you criticize your spouse you are also criticizing your offspring of that spouse.

Be careful to avoid *name calling* in your family. As certainly as you attach a label to your child, she will tend to feel that that's how she must be. That form of destructive criticism is going to destroy a child's self-esteem.

Placing blame is another self-esteem wrecker. When your child has done wrong, she needs to learn confession, restitution, and forgiveness. If she feels guilty, she will believe that she can never be good enough. Avoid discipline that lays shame or guilt. Focus on redemption and learning to be better.

Combining criticism with praise is another self-esteem destroyer. If your spouse constantly says, "I like you, but I wish you were more . . . " pretty soon you would not remember any of the positive comments. Children need to have discipline and guidance in learning how to act and how to do things, but they need to have that done separately from the praise.

Disapproving of your child's friends is another sure way of hurting her self-esteem, so try very hard to accept those friends and let them enter into your family's life in a positive way. Then your child will know that you approve of her choices. Of course, if certain friends are clearly damaging to your child, you will need to help her discern the problems there.

I hope, parents, that you will avoid these enemies of self-esteem, and that as you develop your own self-confidence as parents you will transmit this to your children.

HEROES

What kind of influence do heroes have?

Many years ago, heroes tended to be local people like the family doctor or the mayor. Later, heroes came from books, and the books a child read would provide him with role models.

But in today's world the heroes are the well-paid sports stars, weird video musicians, and television celebrities. Some heroes are even characters in gross animated TV sitcoms.

While some sports stars or TV personalities are truly good and generous people, the majority are not. They are heroes not because of what they have achieved or what causes they espouse but simply because they are rich celebrities.

A true hero is one who manifests higher values like integrity, generosity, kindness, compassion, honesty, industry, gentleness, love, and faith. A hero is someone who, forgetting his own needs, lives for God and the good of others.

Parents can help children find good heroes by introducing them to high-quality literature, renting videos of some of the classics of literature and history, and buying videos that exhibit Christian values. Local libraries often carry children's audio and video tapes that focus on good heroes, such as great musicians of the past or characters in great literature. Public television stations also carry programs that offer children images of truly heroic people of many different races. And Christian bookstores carry a wide range of books and tapes that offer children superstars that are truly good models.

POLITENESS

What's the key to raising children who are sincerely polite?

The basis of all manners and politeness is a loving concern for the well-being of other people. If parents can somehow convey that to their children, they will have solved the major part of the politeness issue. Children need to learn (and can learn) an awareness of their own feelings and how to keep them positive, loving, and considerate. They need also to learn to be sensitive to the needs and feelings of other people, so that they can respond in a considerate and thoughtful way.

Good manners are expressed in saying *please* or *thank you* or *excuse me* and in not considering one's own comfort or wishes ahead of other people's. Teaching manners to children can be done through modeling as you express please and thank you as husband and wife and to your children. You will be teaching them to use those same good manners back to you, and in turn with other people.

Sometimes modeling and verbally teaching a child to use good manners are not enough. There are times when children simply do not want to say the right things, and in that case you may need to use discipline; for example, if your child refuses to say please, he should not get the item he desires.

UNPOPULAR CHILD

If you can see that your child is unpopular, should you step in and do something?

I think that I would. It's obvious that every child can't be the most popular in the class. But it can hurt when your boy or girl is left out. Being well-liked reinforces a child's sense of significance and self-worth. It's fun to be popular and part of a group of friends. There's security in belonging. Being well-liked also gives children the opportunity to influence their peers, which results in a sense of power.

On the other hand, being popular can become a goal in itself, and a child can be driven to try to be as well liked as possible. In doing so, she can lose the individuality and personal values that are essential to later maturity and integrity. Being popular can actually cause a sense of insecurity when one fears losing her position in a group. But by far the worst risk is that a child's sense of worth can become dependent on status and belonging to a group. A child's self-worth should come from inside where she knows she is a loved and valued person. What, then, is a parent to do about a child who is not well liked?

1. *Check out how your child relates to others.* Be sure that your child is kind, thoughtful, and empathetic with other children, not selfish and demanding. If your child lacks social skills, teach her how to play with other children, how to talk with other children, and how to be a considerate and thoughtful friend. A good book for this is *"Nobody Likes Me": Helping Your Child Make Friends* by Elaine McEwan. It has a chapter to instruct kids in basic social skills.

2. *Evaluate your child's personality.* Some children are quieter and more introverted. They simply prefer being alone. They are not lonely. They like their own company, and they are very satisfied to have only one or two friends. If this is the case, don't force your child to belong to a large group, and avoid communicating that there is something wrong with having fewer friends. But do be concerned if she has *no* friends.

12

PHYSICAL DEVELOPMENT

LEFT- OR RIGHT-HANDED?

Our two-and-a-half-year-old daughter sometimes seems to be right-handed but uses her left hand for things like holding a fork or spoon. My question is, should she have a dominant hand by this age, or is it still developing? Is there anything we should do to help her?

Handedness is an important issue to parents, because ours is still truly a right-handed world. Children who grow up to be left-handed adults can have some difficult times in using right-handed equipment.

Hand dominance is not truly established until perhaps five or even six years of age in many children. Sometimes it happens earlier, when a child is strongly right-handed or left-handed, but much more commonly children start out life being ambidextrous. That means they can use one hand one time and the other another time, with equal skill. As children grow, you can help them function in our right-handed world by encouraging them to use the right hand when possible. It is equally important, however, not to *force* that to happen. The motor area of the brain is very close to the speech center of the brain. Forcing a child to change the motor activity from the left to right hand can cause problems in the speech area of the brain. There are, however, ways to encourage right-hand use without making it a serious problem. And encouraging this can help a child later in life if it means that he or she, though left-handed, can better survive in a right-handed world.

When the child is quite small and an item is handed to her, place it in her right hand. When the child picks up something with the left hand that she may use for a period of time, gently try placing it in her right hand. Help her to transfer that item from the left to the right hand while she is still young enough to use it with equal skill in either hand. If your child shows a clear inclination for the left hand, allow it. Avoid turning a healthy sort of supervision into a power struggle by forcing your child to change handedness, which simply is not healthy.

It can also be important to look at your child's feet. A great many parents are not aware that their child may be right- or left-footed. As your child is crawling, notice which foot or knee the child crawls on first. Watch on which foot she puts a sock or shoe first. Which foot does she start out with when she is running? It is helpful to try to get your child to correlate right-handedness with right-footedness, and vice versa, rather than having a mixed dominance of one foot and the opposite hand. However, don't worry excessively over things that nature itself will determine.

HEALTH CHECKUPS

Those visits to the doctor can really be expensive.

With that in mind, how often do you think a seemingly healthy boy or girl needs a checkup?

A baby needs a very thorough examination at birth to be certain that there are no problems that need treatment. Your pediatrician should then give you a schedule of "well baby" visits which include checkups and immunizations. If you cannot afford checkups with your doctor, then call your local visiting nurse association to see about obtaining checkups and immunizations inexpensively through them or some other organization.

Ordinarily, the baby should be seen again within six to eight weeks of birth unless problems occur earlier.

After that six weeks' checkup, the child will need an examination again at about four and six months of age. Every child should be immunized against whooping cough, tetanus, diphtheria, measles, mumps, polio, and probably menningitis (the HIB vaccine) and hepatitis. These immunizations (in the form of shots or liquid medicine) protect the child against these dangerous diseases.

Currently there is a lot of concern regarding a rare but possibly serious reaction to the whooping cough (DTaP or DPT) vaccine. The likelihood of an infant's getting this severe and sometimes fatal disease is much greater than the chance of a reaction. Therefore, parents should not refuse the pertussis (whooping cough) portion of the DTaP shot unless there is a good reason to do so. Speak with your doctor.

Beyond immunizations, regular checkups for a child allow a physician to carefully monitor the child to be sure that there is no abnormality of the endocrine system or a premature closing of the bones of the skull. That could hamper the child's brain development. After six or seven months of age an annual visit for a checkup is usually adequate for a typical child.

DENTAL CARE

When do parents need to start their children on a dental-care program?

A dentist friend of mine tells me that as soon as a baby's teeth begin to erupt, dental care should begin. Although baby teeth are only temporary, they should still be protected from decay. And this is not hard. Even a child of just a few months can have his teeth swabbed with a soft cotton cloth (no toothpaste) before bed. Milk leaves a film on babies' teeth, and that film encourages the growth of the bacteria that cause tooth decay. That is one reason pediatricians warn parents not to put a child to bed with a bottle of milk or juice. If a child must have a bottle at bedtime, it should be water only.

A child's diet is also very important in providing good tooth development and preventing decay. Too many starches and sugars or highly refined, soft diets leave tiny particles of food in the mouth that promote bacterial growth. Rougher foods that contain whole grains and crusts can help to rub off the film that collects and may prevent some of the particle deposits that cause tooth decay. The old adage, "An apple a day keeps the doctor away" works for the dentist as well. Try eating an apple sometime when you've not brushed your teeth. You will find that after you eat that apple, your teeth feel clean and fresh. There is an enzyme in the apple that actually cleans teeth, so to help promote good tooth care give your child plenty of fruit, particularly apples. Don't give raw apples or whole grapes to a baby or toddler, though, because they can cause choking.

Older children should brush their teeth after every meal to remove food particles and to toughen their gums. When they are in school, brushing twice a day is adequate. Use fluoride toothpaste and provide small, soft brushes for plenty of brushing time without hurting the child's gums. Teach them to spit out the toothpaste, not swallow it, as it is not meant for eating!

Flossing a child's teeth is important, too. The in-between tooth surfaces certainly are cleaned best with floss.

A child's first visit to the dentist should come somewhere between his second and third birthdays. He can just go along with you on a regular visit or with some other relative who has a relaxed, positive attitude towards dentists. Your child should become familiar with the dentist's office, and the dentist should speak to him personally about dental care. Then when regular visits begin—perhaps about age three—the child will not be afraid of the dentist's office.

PROPER MATTRESS

My granddaughter is still sleeping in a crib, but her parents are getting ready to put her in a regular bed. They are planning on a waterbed. I'm wondering if it is healthy for children to sleep on waterbeds.

I understand that waterbeds can actually have some benefits for children. However, the support of a well-constructed mattress is quite adequate for most children. The only exception I can imagine is those who might have special orthopedic problems that would require an unusually firm bed.

When should a baby leave her crib and go into a bed? I would recommend anywhere between two and five years of age. Some babies prefer the security of the crib for quite some time. Others, the more active ones, start climbing down when they still seem small enough to be in a crib. The important point is that the baby be in a bed that is safe and comfortable. If the child is climbing out of the crib, then it is time to get rid of it. You do not want the child falling out of the crib while trying to get down. "Toddler beds" are small frames that use the crib mattress, sit close to the floor, and take up less room than a regular single bed. These beds can be used by children for several years, and they save the expense of buying a new mattress.

SHOES

Do you think it's necessary to buy expensive shoes for children? One of the reasons I've avoided the discount places is because they are self-service, and I'm not really sure how to pick out shoes that fit.

Sometimes better shoes (or more expensive ones) are necessary, yet those times are fairly rare. Most children have such average feet that any shoes or no shoes are perfectly fine. Those children who have orthopedic problems will demand special fitting. Watch your child's feet, therefore, to see if they tend to toe out or in. Notice the child's ankles as he walks. See if the ankles collapse inward or if the child walks on the outer edge of the foot. If you can't tell that for sure by watching the child walk, notice where the shoes tend to wear. If they wear on the inner sole, then it is possible that the child's ankles or arches are weak. If the outer part wears off sooner, then the child's foot may be rolling outward in a way that can create problems later on. If you have concerns, ask your pediatrician. He or she may refer you to an orthopedic doctor who will decide if the child's feet need special orthotic devices or different shoes. If you are unsure about shoes, certainly go to a shoe store that caters to children and have a well-trained salesperson fit your child's feet.

Otherwise, you can fit your child's shoes yourself. It's best to shop for shoes in the afternoon or evening, when feet may be swollen. When the shoe is on the foot, the child's new shoe should be a *thumb's width too long*. That means that if you press down where the child's big toe is, your thumb should fit between the big toe and the end of the shoe. It should be about *half a finger's width* (or the edge of your finger) *too wide* as you press the edge of your finger between the little toe and the edge of the shoe. You should have enough room to feel that finger settle into leather or fabric at that point. This gives room for your child's foot to spread a little and to grow enough to get reasonable wear out of the shoe without its being so large that it creates blisters or discomfort from friction. When you go to an expensive regular shoe store with a shoe salesperson, watch how he or she fits your child, and you will learn some of the techniques for buying at least some of your child's shoes in a less-expensive store.

CONTACT LENSES

At what age would you consider getting contacts for a child?

That is a problem that I have had to contend with personally, because all of my children wear glasses. My experience is, however, that very few eye doctors will recommend contacts for children younger than twelve to fourteen. Twelve, in fact, is quite early. Soft contacts are safer than the hard ones, but even soft contacts have some risks.

There are several issues that can help parents to know how to choose the time for contacts. First of all, the degree of visual impairment is important, and children who are extremely nearsighted benefit most from contacts. Because contacts go directly over the eyes, the vision is better, the convenience greater, and the child may believe she looks better without glasses.

Another issue to consider is a child's level of responsibility. Contacts take a great deal of care. They can be lost; they are expensive; they must be kept clean in order to avoid infections or injury to the eye. If your child is not very responsible, you may find that neither you nor the child can afford the luxury of contact lenses. Even with great care, contact lenses can cause damage to the cornea of the eye.

A third issue is your child's activity level. Children who are in swimming or other active sports are much more likely to have their contact lenses damaged, lost, or broken. Broken contact lenses in the eye can cause irreparable damage.

A final issue is the degree of social stigma that wearing glasses causes. In earlier grades, wearing glasses can make a child seem more glamorous to her friends or can cause her to be teased. The teasing, however, can usually be dealt with by teaching the child a clever response to offer children who make fun of her. But in the later grades, especially high school, glasses can seriously affect a child's sense of self-esteem.

Ask your eye doctor to recommend the right time and the way your child may move from glasses to contact lenses. Look into insurance policies for contacts during the active, growing-up years when they can be readily lost. Your child's vision is priceless. Take good care of it.

HOW MUCH SLEEP?

I am the mother of a growing three-and a-half-year-old, and I want to know how much sleep my little boy needs. Also, can he still be expected to take a nap?

Believe it or not, little babies up to the age of almost six months need eighteen to twenty hours of sleep a day. There is a rather rapid decline in the amount of sleep that's needed after that time. While every child should get *at least* eight hours of sleep, there are factors that affect whether they need more. This can guide you in establishing bedtimes for your children.

The *age and growth rate* of a child certainly are important factors. I've already described the amount of sleep that little babies need. By the early grades, they need much less, and in adolescence they may revert to needing more again. As children grow rapidly, they need more rest.

A child's *health* will affect the amount of sleep as well. Children who have allergies or upper respiratory infections, colds, fevers, or any other illness, will need more sleep than children who are in good health.

There is an inborn energy generator that also helps to determine how much sleep is needed. The amount of *energy* that's expended on a daily basis can influence the amount of required rest.

If your child is getting enough sleep, then he will awaken in the morning in plenty of time for school. If you have to awaken him regularly, or if he has to use an alarm in the early grades, then he needs to go to bed earlier at night.

Each child's brain and body will bring about drowsiness when he is tired. You will get used to the signs (like irritability or drooping eyelids) that indicate your child is tired. Many babies give up their morning nap by one year of age. Children often stop their afternoon naps at the age of three or four, though some continue through kindergarten. Often children this age will have difficulty going to sleep at night if they have had an afternoon nap.

Eight to ten hours of sleep per night into early puberty is usually plenty, and during puberty nine or ten hours is none too much. Keep bedtime a snuggly, warm, and intimate time—a time for the exchange of love and confidence, nurturing, and prayers. Don't let it become a power struggle.

SPEECH PROBLEMS

How can parents decide if their boy or girl has a speech problem serious enough to merit attention?

Many speech problems of children are temporary. For instance, I heard of a little boy who simply would not talk. The parents came to the doctor repeatedly, asking for help. He checked the boy's palate and tongue and every area of the child's body to find out why he was not talking. He was mentally capable of talking. He was sent to various speech pathologists for a diagnosis and evaluation, and no one could find anything wrong. But when that boy turned six and went to first grade, he began talking and has barely stopped ever since!

One speech concern, then, is that of *delayed speech.* When a child has reached three or four years of age and is not talking, parents need to wonder. Medical professionals do not worry about a speech delay until that time, however, because some children simply do not talk much before then. If the child shows other evidence of problems, such as not responding when spoken to, then a checkup is required to rule out a hearing problem.

The second speech concern is *abnormal sounds.* The child who lisps and pronounces *s* as if it is *th,* or who confuses *r* and *l* as well as other sounds, will cause his parents to worry. Many abnormal sounds are related to hearing baby talk from parents, even when the child is no longer small. Most children will outgrow this habit when adults routinely stop the baby talk. My speech pathologist consultant says that parents need not worry about abnormal sounds until eight or nine years of age. If the baby sounds persist through that time, a speech therapist should evaluate the child. Most public schools provide well qualified speech therapists, so take advantage of this resource.

Stuttering and stammering is a serious condition that worries many people. A friend of mine indicated that his boy began stammering so badly he could not get a sentence out. He and his wife took the child to a speech pathologist. As the pathologist worked with them and the little boy, she discovered that the child, being the youngest of the family, was not able to get anyone's attention when he wanted to talk. So he learned to stutter in order to keep the center stage once he did get it! Despite doubting that this was the problem, the family followed her recommendation, which was to give the child plenty of time to talk and plenty of attention. He overcame his difficulty very quickly.

A refusal to speak because of anger or fear is not uncommon. We call that *elective mutism*. If that is to be corrected, both the child and the parents must have the help of a professional.

Almost all children learn to talk. They may talk too much or too little. They may talk with a little difficulty, but the important fact for you to remember is that communicating the love and concern you feel is what really counts.

PLASTIC SURGERY

If you could afford to give your child either a better education or a better-looking face, which would you choose?

I am assuming here that the question is being asked about a child with a truly disfiguring flaw. I definitely believe that a better education will benefit a child more than a handsome face. Becoming a productive person offers much more meaning and purpose in life than having a good appearance.

Therefore, if you are asking about surgery simply to reduce a large nose or sharpen a weak chin, then I believe you ought to ask yourselves some questions. Who is it that judges whether a child's appearance is good or bad? Sometimes, because of certain familial traits or values, parents can be overly sensitive about certain aspects of appearance. For example, if you were teased about your nose as a child, you will be especially sensitive to your son's feelings if he has the same nose. Also, different cultures look for different types of beauty. In the U.S., we might think a child's nose too big or the jaw too small. Yet in parts of Europe a large nose is often seen as a sign of distinction. So, you need to think about whether your child's problem is a real one or one that's related to family or community values.

Further, parents ought to examine how abnormal their child really is in comparison with his or her friends. Is the child feeling inferior or inadequate because of a characteristic or a handicap that may be corrected? It is rare, in my experience, to find children who are so unusual that they stand out as being ugly.

If your child does have a significant disfigurement, such as scarring from burns or a prominent birthmark, let me suggest what you may do for your child:

1. Go to a physician and talk about the issue. Is surgery recommended? How much will it cost? Is it possible that by having a psychiatric evaluation and determining how seriously the problem affects your child's emotional health that your insurance may cover the cost of plastic surgery?

2. Is there a nonsurgical way to correct the problem? Many children can enhance their appearance by cosmetic means, such as getting a new haircut, wearing a certain type of clothing, or, as they get older, wearing contact lenses or corrective makeup.

If corrective procedures are impossible or you cannot afford to have them done, then you need to help your child to understand that this disfigurement is part of what makes him or her unique. It is something that will cause some grief, but the child can get through that grief and move on to understanding that appearances are not all there is. As your child learns to compensate for limits in one area, he or she will develop a greater sense of strength in other areas. Developing academic skills, social skills, and activities that can be shared with other children can more than compensate for the heartache of having a significantly flawed appearance. Teach your child to use her own pain to learn compassion for others. And teach your child that all of us, to each other and to God, are beautiful when we are beautiful on the inside. Even the most glamorous model is ugly when the heart is full of evil.

13

SEXUAL CONSIDERATIONS

BIRDS AND BEES

My mother and father never talked to me about sex. Now I am the father of a young son. Is this something I should do or that my wife should take care of?

Both you *and* your wife should be involved in teaching your child about the birds and the bees—and the rest of his sex education. However, you as father and mother should begin with yourselves. Talk about your child and what you want him to know about sex, especially what you want him to know about his own sexuality. Begin by asking yourselves this question: What kind of a man, husband, and father do I want him to become? Discuss this question until you are comfortable with it.

Be aware that each parent teaches a child about this. Mothers give sons a special slant on how women view them and what a woman is like. Fathers need to be models to their sons and examples to their daughters of how men ought to behave towards women. One person alone cannot give full sex education to a child. It takes two.

From discussing your values and what it is you want your child to learn, go on to actual teaching. Many people have made jokes for so long about "the birds and the bees" that they forget that it's a wonderful way to begin—teaching your young child how bees carry pollen from one flower to another, thereby fertilizing that flower and making it possible for it to bear seed.

How is it that birds lay and hatch eggs? How is it that birth takes place in the lives of pets within the family? These are simple, natural ways of teaching your child about sex. Keep the information that you give your child simple, direct, to the point, and appropriate to his age. Be calm, natural, loving, and keep the door open for future communication. You can help your child to grow up with a wholesome attitude and identity as a sexual being.

SEX EDUCATION TIMING

What help can you offer to parents who don't want to give their children more sexual information than they need, but do want to keep ahead of what's on television and what other kids are offering?

It hurries any parent to stay ahead of television and their children's peers! Many children have too much sexual information far too early. The most important guide I can give parents is that they set a climate that encourages the child to question any area of her life, including sexual issues. Whenever she is concerned or interested or hears a confusing comment, she should feel free to talk about such issues with you. You must look for avenues through which to teach. Start where it is easy. We have become so sophisticated that the simple means of teaching children about sex has been forgotten. Those simple facts about biological procreation are a wonderful beginning to understanding human sexuality.

CHECKPOINTS FOR SEX EDUCATION

What are the attitudes about sex children should have learned by the time they reach school age?

There are six in all, and they begin with the parents.

1. Good body image: A child's attitude towards her body is an important element in sexuality. If the child feels that the sexual parts of her body are shameful, and she is embarrassed by them, then she will come to marriage later on with inhibitions and misconceptions that can make her sexual relationship unhappy. Teach your child that *her body is beautiful,* that God made it, and that she needs to value it and give it dignity and pride. Obviously not being ashamed does not mean that a child flaunts her body or exposes herself to others.

2. Open attitude: Children need to have an *open, accepting, and honest attitude toward sex.* That attitude, parents, comes from you. I have worked with many families in which the parents were so ashamed to talk about sexuality that the child could not have an open, unashamed attitude. You need to talk with one another, read wholesome books, and share your ideas with trusted friends until you become comfortable with your feelings about sexuality.

3. Accurate information: I find many families do not have a vocabulary with which to discuss sexual issues. You need to learn the *names for the various parts of the body,* as well as their functions. Any junior-high health textbook or encyclopedia can provide those.

4. Respect for privacy: Teach your child to *respect the*

privacy of others and expect it in return. Many children investigate one another's bodies out of curiosity, but this can result in exploring that frightens the child. You need to teach your child not only to respect, admire, and appreciate her own body, but to respect others' privacy as well.

5. Respect for self: Your child also deserves privacy and dignity. Her *body is her own,* and no one has the right to touch it without her permission. Most schools now have a program called "Good Touch, Bad Touch" that helps children distinguish between loving touches and touches that violate their privacy and lead to sexual abuse. Reinforce this teaching at home so your child will not be exploited.

6. Awe of God's creation: Teach your child to *approach the human body with awe* for God's creation. The "bottom line" of all these attitudes is that sexuality and the human body are God's creations, and they were created to be good.

FAMILY NUDITY

Do you think there is any harm in having my two-year-old daughter and her seven-year-old brother take their baths together? And what about letting them in the room when their dad and I are dressing or bathing?

Parents need to keep an emphasis on naturalness when young children bathe together. Sexuality, and male and female bodies, are gifts from God to be appreciated and protected. Children should not be taught to feel shame about their naked bodies. But they should be taught that their bodies are their own, not to be touched or exploited by anyone.

Bathing children together can be a neat way to allow them to see the boy/girl differences. However, as a parent, you ought to be present when children bathe together in order to prevent an unwholesome preoccupation with the sexual parts of their bodies. If they ask questions about the differences between them, calmly explain them. And comply promptly when a child asks to begin to bathe privately.

The question of whether children should see their parents unclothed is a common one. Many parents go around the house without much on in the presence of their children. This has had no harmful effect whatsoever. On the other hand, if parents do not normally do this, then a child may express surprise if he suddenly comes upon a scantily dressed parent. Take your cue from your child. If it bothers the child, then I suggest that you practice privacy. In today's sexually focused culture, I tell parents to weight their decisions toward privacy.

TOUCHING MOMMY

Over the past few months my four-year-old has become extremely preoccupied with my breasts—both when I am undressed and when I am clothed. I don't want her to think of this as ugly or forbidden, and yet I don't want her interest to continue. She saw me breastfeeding over a year ago and was not at all interested then.

Many three- and four-year-olds develop an interest in Mommy's breasts. In my experience, this almost always relates to a time that they have seen their mother or another mother nursing a baby. Even though this was a year ago, the child would not have forgotten that experience, and there may be some special reason why she is renewing her interest now.

Frankly, I see this as a natural curiosity. It gives parents a wonderful chance to explain the purpose of a mother's breasts and ask for any questions she may have about Mother's body. A little girl may be curious about why she is a girl and yet she doesn't have breasts. Explain to her that someday she will develop breasts, and help her to ~~know~~ how and when that will happen. With either a boy or a girl, it is important to recognize that you know they like the feel of soft things, and being a soft mommy is part of the cuddling that all children and parents enjoy. Explain frankly, however, that you simply do not feel good about being touched or stroked on that part of your body—either alone or in front of other people.

DOLLS FOR BOYS

My little boy is three and a half. At a very early age, he showed an interest in dolls, so I gave him a doll to play with, thinking I ~~was~~ doing the right thing. Now I'm wondering if I made a big mistake. He senses that his father and I are uptight about it. Do you have any advice for me?

This is not an uncommon problem, and actually I would like to address it in two parts. The first issue is fairly simple. That is whether or not boys should be allowed to play with dolls. Honestly, I am in favor of boys playing with dolls because I believe it will help them to learn how to be good daddies. In not playing with dolls, many men have failed to learn basic parenting skills.

I suggest, however, that Daddy show the little boy how to play with dolls the way fathers play with little babies. This will give the child a masculine technique, rather than a feminine or motherly technique in playing with those dolls.

EFFEMINATE SON

I'm getting worried about my ten-year-old son. I've caught him dressing up in my women's clothes, and

he seems to thoroughly enjoy it. Am I overreacting? Can you help me know what to do?

Many boys dress up in girls' or women's clothing at times, such as at Halloween. That is quite a different issue than the one addressed by this mother. This mom, and others like her, is concerned about her son's habitual preference for feminine items. This can lead to a problem when the child reaches puberty and is searching for a sexual identity.

So, first, make sure you have a loving, happy relationship with your son. Sometimes children dress in their parents' clothes in order to feel close to them. Is there a chance that your son is seeking a closer relationship with you?

Second, I would make sure that he has access to some soft, silky men's shirts. He may just enjoy the texture of your clothes. Or perhaps he does not have access to men's clothes. Allow him to dress up in Daddy's clothes, or get him some hand-me-downs from adult male friends. Let him try out the big shoes, hats, jackets, or shirts.

Third, ensure that your son spends time with his Dad. Have Dad take time to teach him what he does at work. Have your son help Dad clean the car or the family room, mow the grass, go fishing, cook, do the laundry, or whatever Dad does.

Fourth, if Dad is not an active part of your son's life, check whether he has a warm, positive relationship with some other significant male. Include in your family activities other male relatives or adult friends who can be good role models for him. So long as this man is respectful of your son, affirming, and never abusive or intrusive, you should encourage the relationship and make sure your son has time to see this friend.

Do not punish or disapprove of your son's effeminacy. That will drive it into hiding and cause guilt and fear. He may be afraid that he is different from other people and that something is wrong with him. As his mother, you need to understand his needs for approval, closeness, warmth, and softness.

Avoid overreacting. Simply encourage masculinity in your son. Teach him to open doors for you and to carry things for you. Be proud of his masculine traits, and reflect them to him in compliments. Find ways to turn his effeminate tendencies into sensitive masculinity. Your son can grow in his own unique way into manhood, and you can be very proud of him.

DAD NEEDED

I'm a single parent, and my two girls do not see their father much due to distance and his ongoing problems. How important is it for them to be close to a dad?

Dads are vitally important in the lives of both boys and girls. Girls need Dad's pride and delight in them if they are to have the healthy sense of self-worth they need. When Dad is involved in her life, a girl is significantly more likely to be motivated and successful in school, sports, and just about any other aspect of her life. Furthermore, it is through Dad's example that she learns about men and how to love and respect them, and how to choose a good husband if she decides to marry.

A child who does not have an involved father would benefit from building a close relationship with another adult male. This could be Grandpa or an uncle, or it could be a friend or neighbor. Be sure that the man is respectful of her affection, positive, and never abusive nor intrusive, and that male friend can be a valuable adopted member of the family.

DELAYED/EARLY PUBERTY

What are the worries for a teen who may mature either earlier or later than his or her peers?

The preadolescent and adolescent years can be difficult, even under the best of circumstances. That difficulty can be multiplied for the boy or girl whose biological clock is a bit off from the majority. Any differences certainly carry their own set of problems.

Early or late puberty is more obvious in girls because of their breast development (or lack thereof) and menstrual cycles. Girls who develop as early as ten or eleven commonly feel as if they have been unfairly pushed into an adult world for which they feel unprepared. They feel different from their peers and almost have a sense of being abused. Young girls become embarrassed when they have their periods. If they have an accident in school, they do not know how to handle it. They need help from parents and teachers to prevent such accidents and to protect their privacy.

Some people believe that early puberty causes an early preoccupation with sexual interests, but I disagree. Sexual awareness is an issue, and one that demands consideration by parents to prevent a child's precocious or excessive fascination with sexual interests. But early puberty does not equate with early sexual interest.

Girls who develop late will also face consequences, especially if their chests remain flat when all their peers are sporting filled-out bras. Such a girl may struggle with poor self-esteem and may have to put up with some cruel jokes or teasing, especially in gym class. Like any child with an unusual characteristic, this girl should be taught to respond flippantly and proudly to those who make fun of her, thereby letting the wind out of the sails of her teasers. Something like "Did you know that _____ (plug in the name of the latest supermodel) did not wear a bra till she was much older?" could stop the comments and communicate that this flat-chested girl is not to be tangled with.

Boys, too, may be late bloomers. And they have as much of

a problem as the girls who find the advent of their puberty early. Boys who remain short, whose voices do not change as soon as their friends, who do not develop hair growth and other signs of masculinity with their friends, often feel left out, inadequate, different, and can develop a serious inferiority complex. Again, you might want to help your son by looking up facts about famous athletes who were (or are) short and giving him this as ammunition to use if attacked by teasers.

Boys who develop early tend not to face as many consequences as girls who develop early because the boys' puberty is not so easily recognized. Boys who are tall and manly tend to receive more respect than their younger-seeming peers. However, these boys may struggle to accept their sexual feelings, becoming embarrassed by wet dreams and aroused desires. Boys need to be taught by their parents that these events are normal and expected.

If you believe that your child is not developing normally, have him or her examined and let your doctor decide whether there is a hormonal imbalance or other need for concern. If your child is concerned, the physician can reassure him or her. Don't let your child feel different or inadequate because of his or her particular clockwork. Instead, if your child wants to compensate, help him or her to dress and groom in a way that will make up for the differences in development and enable the child to fit better into the social sphere of peers.

SEXUAL PEER PRESSURE

In your counseling, do you see teenagers who are feeling pressure to be sexually active?

It's a sad fact that teenage pregnancies are extremely common, and sexually transmitted diseases are epidemic. Whether we like to admit it or not, even teens from "good" families are not insulated from pressures to be sexually active. They can be made to feel almost abnormal if they are not as experienced as their classmates. One study revealed that over 45 percent of regularly churched youth have had sex before completing high school.

A very good friend of mine happens to be a teacher, and she came home from school one day to find her own eighth-grade daughter in a risky situation with a young man she was dating. When my friend talked with her daughter about this and what could have happened, the child said, "But, Mother, I'm the only one of my friends who has never had sex." I think it was sad that a fourteen year old should have to say that, but it was true.

Peers are very important to adolescents. I find a great many children (and literally they are "old" children) feeling lonely. Out of their loneliness, they have a need for companionship that very quickly can become physical rather than just social. One girl I worked with some years ago felt that because she was so lonely, she owed anyone who paid her any attention—even the purchase of a soft drink after school—a sexual favor in return.

The push of young people into premature adulthood is common today. There's too much information available to young people much too soon. There is too little comfortable openness with parents. Talking about questions and feelings and finding thoughtful answers within the family is not very common. There is far too much exposure to sexually stimulating sights and ideas on television and in magazines. Local grocery stores or drugstores often display explicit materials on open shelves, available to anyone.

The recreational attitude about sex—that it's simply something for fun—detracts from this very beautiful, significant part of life.

I suggest that parents forbid real "dating" until at least age fifteen. By then teens have developed some self-awareness and a degree of maturity. Talk *with* them (not *at* them) about establishing wholesome dating practices focused on healthy activities. While recognizing their feelings, help them identify ways to avoid sexually stimulating places while controlling sexual impulses. Keep an open, nonjudgmental, interested but not controlling attitude, and your teens will be open with you.

There are a number of groups (such as "True Love Waits") that are promoting celibacy and the saving of sex for marriage. A few contemporary Christian musicians and athletes also encourage purity. And many churches sponsor youth groups that aim to help young people resist sexual temptation and encourage them to conduct their social lives in groups instead of couples. Teens will benefit from finding friends who share their values and beliefs and who will not treat them as weirdos if they are not sexually active. Help your teen to find those friends and offer him or her the means to socialize with them.

14

HOLIDAYS AND ENTERTAINMENT

HOLIDAY PREPARATION

How can we make family holidays really special?

The following elements are so important, and unfortunately it's very easy to unknowingly miss them all.

Mood. I like to try to set a mood of general congeniality. The goodwill that is so essential to holidays is vital in the family as well. Smiles, laughter, and jokes are important all through the year, but holiday time is a natural time for such goodwill and happiness, as well as tempting secrets and surprises. The inclusion of children in the decorating, baking, and other preparations is sometimes a bit of a trial to a busy mother, but it is also a part of the happiness in building family traditions.

Rest. Holidays should also be a time of quiet and peacefulness. Take time out personally and as a family to be quiet and to look at the decorations and enjoy the packages of anticipation.

Meaning. Meditate on the real meaning of God's gifts of his Son to our world. And thank God for the other gifts he gives us, such as good food, warm houses, and families. The ultimate expression of holiday sharing is in the free gifts of God.

Tradition. Building traditions is so essential! Every Thanksgiving we have a similar menu for dinner and breakfast. At Christmas, we have familiar tree ornaments, which we have saved from time immemorial, and each year the children and I enjoyed unpacking those ornaments and using them on our traditional tree. Reviving old customs and recipes, which perhaps your grandparents enjoyed, might be helpful to your children in valuing their backgrounds and learning from whence they came.

SANTA CLAUS

If your children were small today, what would you tell them about Santa and Christmas?

What *I* would tell them is very easy for me to answer. Complications sometimes arise, however, when parents have different ideas about Santa Claus. I came from a family who treated Santa as a fantasy and a pretense (though a very enjoyable one!). Some parents come from families where they treasure their early childhood memories and beliefs that Santa was real. So a compromise becomes necessary. In our family, a very interesting thing happened that I'd like to share with you.

Our son was our second child, and when he was about eight years of age, he decided that it was his duty to reveal to his three-and-a-half-year-old sister that Santa really did not exist. A bit irritated at his premature revelation, I said to him, "All right, since you've told her that, now you go ahead and explain it to her." Well, to my amazement, he did a marvelous job! He told her very kindly and gently, as a mature little boy of eight can do, about the beautiful symbolism of Santa Claus. He explained that Santa was not real, but was pretend, and that you could pretend and still have fun. His sister accepted it very calmly and without a single tear.

Actually I think that's the ideal. Explain to children that Santa Claus is a symbol of congeniality and happiness, of secrets and excitement, of suspense and teasing, and of giving. He can become a delightful experience for children. By letting them understand from the beginning that Santa is make-believe, we can separate for our children the beautiful reality of the person of Jesus Christ—that he was and is very real—and in that reality, we can help them to understand the awe and the wonder, the sacredness, the infinity of God's love, the quietness of God's giving, and the quality of his giving that is so unique. I think both aspects are important to children.

EXTENDING CHRISTMAS CHEER

Can children learn to share with others outside the family?

Children often are accused of being very selfish, but they love to give, and can do so with great excitement and genuineness. I recommend that every family select ways of sharing with others. This might be through giving to a disadvantaged family, serving a meal at a shelter, visiting nursing home residents who have no family, or baking cookies and making ornaments for homebound neighbors. Help your children, if you choose to do this, to avoid condescension or pity, and teach them their responsibility in recognizing the needs of others and giving to other people.

Furthermore, I think it's important that children learn how other people celebrate Christmas. You might read about the way people celebrate Christmas across the country and around the world. Many traditions are fascinating. They might be ones that you would like to adopt into your own family. In our community one of the major shopping centers has booths set up by many different foreign exchange students, and in each of those booths are examples of traditional Christmas celebrations in that particular country. Our family has enjoyed going to visit these displays year after year and sharing in the Christmas festivities of other nations. We also like to visit other churches. Swedish, German, Polish, and Mexican churches, to name a few, all have special religious traditions that you can enjoy.

Special meals and recipes—these, too, are traditions that you can build into priceless memories for your family.

CHRISTMAS GIFT SELECTION

What suggestions do you have for parents when they are shopping for children's presents on a budget?

The joy of Christmas can be totally spoiled by your worrying about paying credit-card bills after the holidays. Parents ought to set a budget. If downsizing or other changes have made this a lean year, be sure to sit down with your children and prepare them ahead of time for the fact that Christmas will not be as generous as it might have been in past years.

Plan early, and make some of your gifts if you are able. Some of the most treasured gifts our children received at Christmas were doll clothes that I had designed and fashioned myself, or a hobbyhorse that a relative had made. There are many special gifts that convey the uniqueness of your love and creativity without costing a great deal.

If you do have money to spend, I recommend that you look for gifts that will stimulate your child's creativity and development: building sets, modeling dough, markers or paints, and musical instruments require your child to put something into the enjoyment of the toy and in turn to gain some developmental abilities from playing with the toy.

Also, look at your child's life over the last six months, and think about things that he has truly longed for. Sometimes we give things that we see on the spur of the moment or that the child happens to see on television. But as you look back over the weeks and months, you may remember something that your son or daughter has wanted for a long time. Giving that special gift may eliminate the need for other presents, because the quality of satisfaction that such a longed-for item can produce is wonderful.

Be careful that you don't give so many things that your child cannot honestly appreciate them. On the other hand, don't give so few things that your child may feel deprived. (This, of course, depends upon the child's age, personality, sense of values, and other facts of life upon which you can base your decision.)

Above all, be sure that Christmas is a time for giving love. The gifts you give must symbolize that—or no matter how much you spend, the presents will somehow miss the mark.

CHRISTMAS "ON YOUR OWN"

What help do you have for young parents who are still trying to decide where they'll spend Christmas?

That certainly is not an easy question. The memories that I treasure most of all are those big family gatherings involving several generations. Sometimes, in the hurry to establish a tradition within a young new family, those transgenerational experiences can be lost. So whenever it's possible, I recommend that at least on alternate years or on alternate holidays young families try to spend some of those times with grandparents. The traditions of those grandparents can set the patterns for your own new family and can give wonderfully warm memories to your children. I think my children would agree with me that their memories of time together with cousins, aunts, uncles, and grandparents are very cherished ones.

Sometimes, however, the distances make that impossible. The time and money that it takes to get to the home of a grandparent may be prohibitive. Personally, I think that saving vacation time and saving money are worth the sacrifice to be together on holidays. But circumstances in some families are so difficult that this can't be done.

In that case, I suggest that families invite the grandparents to spend some of the holidays with them. Even if distances and time may make the young couple unable to travel, the grandparents may be able to come to the young family.

The family also might enjoy shopping for or creating special presents for family members far away. And when you cannot have family with you, try "adopting" someone nearby who needs somewhere to go for the holidays. This might be an "adopted" grandparent, a foreign student who must stay at school over the holidays, or a family at your church that is new to the area and whose family is also far away.

PHOTO ALBUMS

Nearly every home has a box or drawer somewhere that holds a wealth of family snapshots. Please tell us what to do with all those pictures!

I'm delighted to do that, because I find that pictures are very important to people. One of the questions that I frequently ask in doing a psychiatric evaluation of a troubled person is this: If there were a fire in your home, what are the things that you would take out of that house? Almost everyone mentions the family photographs. And I think that for most of us, memories and pictures are very important.

I strongly recommend that as mother and father, you set up for each child his or her own special photograph album. In that album, place items and photos from even before birth that you will want her to think about and remember later on. I strongly recommend that you start with the background of your child's life, and put in her photo album the generations preceding her. Any pictures that you have of grandparents or great-grandparents or the old family farm or homestead—whatever might be in your family—start with that, and give your child a sense of her past and her belonging to some particular set of people.

Very important to children are the residences in which they have lived. The average family moves several times while the children are growing up, so that section of the album may be quite sizable! Pictures of the schools, the neighborhood, special spots in which the child may have had fun, would be wonderful ideas to include. Parks and picnics, vacations and toys, those are the things that someday your child can look back upon with pleasure. Another section should be reserved for friends—playmates and the activities they shared—birthday parties and Christmas celebrations, all very important memories.

Include people who have been significant in the child's life: teachers, a special friend, anyone who has been meaningful in the child's growing-up time. Symbols of the child's progress are also meaningful: sports events, school or church performances, science projects, special pets. All of these are memories that your child will treasure as she grows older and perhaps starts her own family. Your children will want to share this special set of memories with their children someday.

BABY-SITTERS

Do you see any problem with hiring the high-school

girl next door to take over when Mom or Dad take a night off?

There is nothing wrong with leaving the children with a sitter *if* you have carefully checked into that sitter's abilities and maturity. There are instances of sitters who have abused or failed to protect children in their care, and you don't want that to happen.

Be sure to screen baby sitters carefully before hiring one. Here are some criteria by which you might judge a good, reliable sitter. The sitter should have:

- a high level of maturity
- good judgment in times of crisis
- enough self-control to never slap or yell at a child
- the ability to control and discipline a child
- willingness to avoid socializing with peers while sitting
- references that can attest to all of the above

You must give your baby sitter clear guidelines about the kinds of discipline that you use and that you would want her to use in case it is needed. The baby sitter needs to have judgment enough to know when to call you and what she can handle in case she cannot reach you. The basic love of children and the ability to be kind and firm and protective are qualities that I would look for in a baby sitter. I'd like to have a baby sitter who is energetic and willing not only to provide basic care, but to play with my child so that the time they spend together is enjoyed by all.

How can you know what a baby sitter is like? I recommend that you request references and call those references to talk with them personally. I suggest you have a sitter spend some time with your child while you are there, and observe carefully what goes on between them. When your child is old enough, ask him or her how the evening went after the sitter is gone. Observe carefully the condition of the house, the sitter, and the child when you return. If you have concerns, come back unexpectedly and pop in on the sitter during the course of an evening out. It may be an inconvenience, but it may serve a good purpose in helping you to know whether you can entrust your child to this person. Trust your instincts! If you have a sense that something is wrong, don't leave your children with that sitter until you have investigated.

Another suggestion that I have is that you might trade baby-sitting now and then, so the cost doesn't become prohibitive. Several couples who are trustworthy friends can relieve one another and thus provide some special time out. And, of course, there are grandparents. The good ones are worth their weight in gold. I know that I love to keep my grandchildren when my daughter goes out!

EVENING OUT

We have a four year old and a new baby. When we go out to a friend's house or to a restaurant in the evening is it better for them to stay at home with a baby sitter or to go with us? We don't mind taking them along, but we wonder if it's too hard on them to go places where they can't talk or play as freely as at home.

That is a good question, and frankly I deplore the practice of always leaving children at home while the parents go out. On the other hand, I know the need of young parents to be free of child-care responsibilities for bits of time through the week. So here are some practical suggestions.

1. Train your children to behave in social situations. Then you can take them along with you and enjoy them, as well as

having your friends enjoy them. Parents might plan some social life at home with their friends in order to train the children. Sometimes this is a real strain on those who must prepare a meal for company, but when spouses help, it can become a delightful family evening.

2. Take children out to family-style or fast-food restaurants now and then, in order to teach them how to behave properly in a social setting. Many family restaurants provide entertainment and special menus for children. If you select your restaurant carefully, you will find this family outing an asset in teaching social skills.

I question, however, if new babies should be taken out. Generally, for the first few weeks they ought to remain at home as their resistance to bacteria is low. After that, if they sleep well in an infant seat and are very calm babies, perhaps you can get by with taking them out for short periods of time. If you take a child to a friend's home, where he or she can be put to bed, then I see no harm in taking young children out for an evening.

The following questions are what you as parents need to answer when deciding whether or not to take out your children: Will the children be able to behave so that you can enjoy your evening out with friends? Will the children be bored? Are they exhausted? Will other people be inconvenienced if your children misbehave? Can *you* enjoyo the evening?

TELEVISION

Watching television is the kind of entertainment that many good parents believe ought to be eliminated from their homes. And yet nearly every family has a set (if not two or three) that is on for a good portion of the day and night. Since television has become such an established part of our homes, do you think it's possible for parents to turn it to an advantage?

Yes, I do, and studies have indicated how we might go about doing that.

Television can help parents teach. We know, for example, that with children who are a little slow in learning to talk, parents can spend time watching a children's program and use the words and images in that program to teach language. Parents can teach their children colors and many other facts by sitting and talking with them about the content of a given program.

Television exposes children to unfamiliar values and experiences. As children grow older, it is possible for parents to teach children about the contrasting values of the world in which we live through television. What is wrong with violence, cheating, promiscuous living, and all of the many other values that television programs espouse? By watching programs with your older children, you can help them to understand what is good and bad about the program itself and about the world that it depicts. You can use television to teach empathy and compassion to your children. For example, you might ask your child, "How would you feel if you were that boy?" or, "What would you have done if you were in a situation like that girl?" Drawing the family together and offering a forum for discussions of all sorts is a positive use of television.

Television can teach sharing. You can use TV to teach your children to share. I recommend that families not have more than one television set. Your children can learn to take turns choosing the programs they want to watch. But kids should not just share with one another. They also need to share the TV with Mom and Dad. Parents sometimes come home from work, wanting to sit and watch the news, but the children are grabbing the television for their own interests. Don't be afraid to teach your children to give you a turn at the TV.

Do be creative as you evaluate your television watching, and decide how you can turn it into a positive influence in your home. And do limit the amount of watching your children do. After school, your kids should have plenty to occupy them the rest of the day without resorting to TV. After homework is done, outdoor activities, reading, crafts, computer learning, and other productive pursuits ought to occupy your child before the TV does. Or, encourage the child to watch educational programs on public television stations and specialized cable channels.

CARTOON VIOLENCE

Do you know the effects of violence in cartoons on young children? My husband and I have four children, ranging in age from two to nine. If you could give me some insight into this subject, I would appreciate it very much.

We in the mental-health profession are concerned about the effect of television violence on children. For many years, studies have indicated that violence does influence young children. One group of school-agers in California was studied a number of years ago after they watched violent scenes, and then they were observed as they played afterward. The children who had watched the violence had a great deal more intensely violent situations among themselves than children who had not watched such scenes. Recently we have learned that even cartoons can have this sort of effect on children. And in the case of cartoons, kids may get the idea that death and injury are not real because cartoon characters get blown up and are perfectly fine a minute later.

Prior to age seven or eight, I think parents must monitor television programs closely. At this early age, children do not have the capacity to determine right from wrong adequately, and they simply do not understand what is good or bad about the cartoons they watch. As you watch television with your child, forbid the violent, destructive programs. Your children will survive without a great deal of television, and there are almost always a few good programs that you can permit. Even with those, I suggest that at times you watch with your children, reinforcing the positive ideals and views portrayed and helping them to understand any questionable views or ideals that are contrary to your own. Kids need to know the truth.

If you are appalled at the kinds of programs that go on the air, write to your local stations or to the program sponsors expressing your views and clearly defining what you see as harmful in those programs.

MUSIC VIDEOS

Our daughter is in her early teens, and she has started watching cable TV stations that air rock videos. Should we be concerned about this?

Yes, indeed! Cable stations that show music videos sometimes air material that is extremely suggestive of violence, explicit sex, and drug abuse. More and more we see physical abuse depicted, accompanied by rap or hard rock music. While these stations also air music videos that are well-done and tasteful, a parent cannot know which type a child is watching unless the parent is watching, too.

I suggest that when a child becomes interested in music videos, a parent watch along with her. Discuss what you see. How does she feel about the scenes of violence or sex or drugs that are portrayed? Is she sensitive to words and pictures that demean women, authority figures, ethnic groups, or the government? In this area, a parent must try to stay informed.

245

VIDEO GAMES

Do you think it's possible that playing video games is harmful to children?

I do think it can be harmful to some children, as these negative effects imply:

- isolation—many video games are not social activities
- neglecting better activities—reading, chores, educational pursuits
- violence—many of the games are actively violent
- intensity—children often seem lost to the world while they play

If you do get video games, select those that develop skill and coordination without violence. Limit the time spent on games, alternating them with more wholesome activities. Watch your children for ill effects, and if you see them, don't hesitate to weed out the video games that might be a cause of those problems. Some children become obsessed with video games, using them as an escape from family troubles or difficulties at school. If you have a child who is constantly glued to a video game instead of socializing with family or friends, you need to make an effort to reconnect with that child and find some more meaningful pursuits for him or her.

However, video games can also be positive influences for:

- family interaction—if parents join in the games
- attracting friends—again, with games for more than one
- developing hand-eye coordination

If your children's friends come to your house to play video games, you can get to know them and how they interact. That's a positive outcome, as it's good to know their friends.

Video arcades are quite a different matter from video games played at home. Such arcades can be undesirable places. A great many drugs are exchanged in public game rooms, alcohol is common, and tobacco smoke is so heavy that one's eyes burn.

I also feel concerned about the money that children spend in such public arcades. There seems to be a compulsive need to play just one more game, with an almost excessive sense of excitement or tension with such activity. Undue competitiveness is a common part of many of these games. Some people argue that this is good, as it allows children to play out their aggression so they do not take it out on their brothers, sisters, or playmates. But such competition may stimulate aggression outside of the arcade.

ROCK CONCERTS

You have a lot of contact with teenagers in your work. What is your opinion on rock concerts and rock music in general?

Many parents are deeply concerned about rock music. A great deal of rock music has to do with promoting the highs of all sorts of drugs along with violence, illicit sex, and crime. Also, each year new methods of exuberant celebration come around, such as "moshing" and "surfing," which have caused a number of injuries and deaths at concerts, parties, and "raves." Parents must try to be informed about these. Many teens are in a desperate search for intense excitement and a means for expressing profound inner anguish. This and the need for social interaction can drive a teen to seek out these exhilarating experiences.

On the other hand, there is some fine contemporary music that has no bad words or criminal influence. In fact, this may be a bridge for many young people from negative, destructive music into more wholesome music and renewed faith in God.

What kind of music your teenager should listen to and whether or not your child should attend a rock concert are certainly important decisions you as parents must make with your child. Get complete information about the group that your young person wants to hear. Be careful that you have accurate information before you make a decision. Being too rigid can prompt your teen to rebel; being too permissive can invite destructive influences. Find a balance.

VALUES CONFLICT

I am a grandmother. I am concerned about my daughter. Each time her own teenage son, who is fourteen, wants to watch something on television that isn't too good, or see a movie rated PG that has bad words in it, they get into a quarrel. I believe in taking a stand, but I wonder if she doesn't overdo it, as she sort of preaches at the child every time this comes up. How do you think she could handle this situation better?

At this time in that child's life, he needs his mother to be more of a friend, not the authoritative parent he needed when he was younger. By discussing issues in a less emotional and more intellectual fashion—much as one would talk with adult friends—this mother will be able to help the teenager express his ideas more openly. This child at fourteen is approaching adulthood and needs to be taught how to think for himself and how to determine what makes something right or wrong, good or bad.

This is one area of life where you must, to be successful, separate emotions from judgment. Discuss movies and TV carefully and clearly with your children. Help them to understand the powerful influence of negative concepts, morals, and values in movies or television programs. That way they will learn to make wise choices on their own.

If you absolutely *must* say no to your teenager, do so kindly. For example, try this approach: "I wish I could give you total freedom. I hate disappointing you. But once in a while I see something really risky in what you want. And I love you enough that I'm willing to suffer your hurt and anger to protect you." I predict this approach will allow you to set adequate boundaries that are rooted in love.

INDEX

RESOURCES

For more information on parenting and related topics, see the author's list of books on page 2 or the following books from Harold Shaw Publishers:

Hancock, Maxine. *Creative, Confident Children: Making the Most of the Preschool Years.*

Holt, Pat, and Grace Ketterman, M.D. *Don't Give In, Give Choices: Winning Your Child's Cooperation.*

_____. *When You Feel Like Screaming: Help for Frustrated Mothers.*

McEwan, Elaine K. *The ABCs of School Success: Nurturing Young Minds.*

_____. *Attention Deficit Disorder: Helpful, Practical Information.*

_____. *Managing Attention and Learning Disorders: Super Survival Strategies.*

_____. *Solving School Problems: Kindergarten through Middle School.*

_____. The Practical Tools for Parents series:

   "I Didn't Do It": Dealing with Dishonesty

   "Mom, He Hit Me": What to Do about Sibling Rivalry

   "Nobody Likes Me": Helping Your Child Make Friends

   "The Dog Ate It": Conquering Homework Hassles

Miller, Kathy Collard. *When Counting to Ten Isn't Enough: Defusing Abusive Anger.*

Miller, Kathy Collard, and Darcy Miller. *Staying Friends with Your Kids.*

Parish, Ruth Ann, M.D. *Your Baby's First Year: Spiritual Reflections on Infant Development.*

To order any of these books, contact your local bookstore.